Early Childhood Units

for the

Alphabet

Written by Sylvia Stone and Holly Bye

Illustrated by Blanca Apodaca-La Bounty and Theresa M. Wright

Teacher Created Materials, Inc.
6421 Industry Way
Westminster, CA 92683
www.teachercreated.com
©1993 Teacher Created Materials, Inc.
Reprinted, 2002, a
Made in U.S.A.
ISBN-1-55734-202-4

Table of Contents

Introduction

The purpose of *Whole Language Units for the Alphabet* is to help children learn to read. Through a variety of activities based on the alphabet, children learn to recognize letters and their sounds. They learn to appreciate literature and understand language structure. They develop skills in listening, speaking, observing, thinking, reading, and writing.

From story apron to finger puppets to related activities and all that is in between, this book is designed to capture children's interest, making learning personal and understandable. It gives the child hands-on experiences in a whole language program.

The story apron is to be used with every letter. It adds fun and mystery. Each letter also has a finger puppet, a related story with lots of alliteration, classroom activities, a word bank, a suggested reading list, a phonics page, and an alphabet page.

A Whole Language Program

A whole language program surrounds children with language. Children are taught the skills of reading, writing, spelling, and speaking through repeated experience with language. These skills are not taught in isolation, but are related to a particular story, book, or poem.

Meaning is emphasized in whole language. The class is immersed in meaning by repeated experiences with the story. It is acceptable and desirable for students to memorize and act out stories. Vocabulary is not introduced and defined before reading the story. The story is read first for enjoyment.

Children are encouraged to create their own stories in a whole language program. They use ideas or patterns from the story to create new stories. Younger children will need lots of direction, modeling, and suggestions from the teacher. The children's stories are often displayed around the classroom. Children enjoy sharing their stories with one another.

In writing their stories, students use approximate or invented spelling. They are urged not to worry about correct spelling, but to sound out the word and spell it as accurately as they can. This will allow them to write frequently and take asks with written language. Older students can correct and edit a second draft.

In a whole language classroom, children are surrounded with print. Walls and bulletin boards are covered with labeled pictures and creative writing. All types of books, including quality children's literature, poetry, magazines, student "published works" and Big Books are available for children to read in the classroom.

Whole language encompasses the total of language use for the child. In every activity the child is made aware of the sounds, letters, and language of each item shown or read and of each action or activity that is done.

Reading with children and allowing them to experience language gives them a good foundation for learning. Through the stories and activities in this book, children will experience language in many different ways. They will have many opportunities to learn and retain the necessary components of language.

How To Use *Whole Language Units for the Alphabet*

Story Apron

The story apron is meant to be used daily. It should have several pockets. Stitching additional pockets to the front of any full length apron such as a cobbler's apron will give you a usable story apron.

Use the apron in teaching the alphabet with the puppets and supporting items.

Before reading the letter's story, put on the story apron. The pockets should have been filled previously with the appropriate finger puppet and items that begin with the same letter. Be consistent in using the story apron. The children will come to know that the apron means something interesting is about to happen. You will have their interest and attention before you begin the lesson.

To introduce a new alphabet letter, take the puppet from its pocket. Say both its letter name and character name. Practice the sound of the letter several times. Read the story. Again practice the letter sound. Say some of the names from the story. Have fun with the tongue-twister quality that some of the names provide!

One by one, take the other items from the apron pockets. Have children say the names of the items. Brainstorm other items that begin with the same letter or, in the case of X, have the sound and letter in it.

Stories

For each letter there is an original story. Each story is about the puppet character and contains many words that begin with the letter that is currently being studied. The words and names in the story are fun and are meant to be repeated many times.

Each story can be used in different ways. The story can be made into a large-size book for use with the entire class. The text of the book can be lettered onto large paper so the children can illustrate the story. Many of the stories can be acted out by the children. Letters and words can be enhanced with these stories. Writing another segment as a sequel to each story can be done as a group or as an individual activity to be shared with all the class.

The children may be interested in writing a song to go along with the story. Be sure to use a familiar tune such as "Row, Row, Row Your Boat" or "Here We Go Round the Mulberry Bush."

The uses listed for the stories are beginning points for you, the teacher. Many other possibilities will appear while using the given suggestions.

How To Use *Whole Language Units for the Alphabet* (cont.)

Word Banks

A word bank is a collection of related words. It grows as a resource. In this case, a letter of the alphabet is studied. Children have a sense of ownership in the word bank as they contribute to the list. This is a quick, fun way for students to integrate reading and writing.

Word banks should be on display in the classroom. Be sure words are large enough to be visible from different areas of the room.

Develop word banks consisting of words children suggest. Write on a large chart and display for all to see. The word bank provided for each letter should be used only when children's repertoire of words has been exhausted.

Each word bank begins with verbs. Encourage children to act out these words. When the children relate the action, beginning sound, and word to the letter being studied, their retention is enhanced. Their knowledge then encompasses their whole language ability.

Activities

Activities are suggested for each letter. These activities help to reinforce the desired letter and sound learning within the useable language of the children.

The suggested activities are many and varied. Consider the age of the children, the space available, and how each activity would fit into the daily schedule as well as other planned lessons when deciding which of the suggested activities to use.

When using each activity, stress the relationship of the activity to the letter that is being studied. Use every opportunity to bring the concept of language, oral and written, into each activity.

How To Use *Whole Language Units for the Alphabet* (cont.)

Suggested Reading Lists

Each letter is accompanied by a Suggested Reading List. The stories on these lists have one or more characters in them that use the letter being studied to begin their names. Read these or other stories and poems with this letter in them as often as possible. The more the children hear the letter sounds and see the letter, the better their retention and incorporation of this portion of language into their entire knowledge.

Alphabet Book Pages

Each letter has a page with a picture that relates to the story. Make copies of these pages for every child. During class have the children color the pages. Keep the pages at school until you complete the entire alphabet. Then show children how to put the pages in order. Assemble the pages into books using a heavy duty stapler. Or punch holes in the pages and assemble with brads or yarn ties. Let the children take the books home to share.

Phonics Activities

Each letter has a related phonics page to be used as a worksheet and/or clothespin game. Reproduce the phonics pages you plan to use as games onto index paper. If a more durable paper is desired, glue a copy of the game to poster or tag board. File folders work well, too. Experiment with colored paper or index paper, to eliminate the need for coloring. As an alterative, ask older student volunteers or teacher aides to color the pictures. Laminate, if possible. For small groups, make several copies of each game.

> **Worksheet:** Make a copy for each child. Direct students to color all of the pictures that begin with the sound of the letter on the page. Allow children to take the pages home and share what they have learned.

> **Clothespin Game:** Duplicate, color, and laminate the phonics pages. Have students clip a clothespin to each picture that begins with the sound of the letter on the page. As a variation, instead of using clothespins, have students make choices with markers such as beans, seeds, or plastic disks.

How To Use *Whole Language Units for the Alphabet* *(cont.)*

Background Cards

Background cards for the finger puppets can be made from 6" x 10" (15cm x 25cm) sheets of poster board. Make one background card for each letter. Using a felt tip pen put a capital and lower case letter near the bottom of each card. At this point you may want to laminate the cards for greater durability.

Measure the puppet against the card to determine how it will fit on the card. Use Velcro® with adhesive back or, with a hot-glue gun, glue a 1/4" (.6cm) piece of velcro tape near the top of the card where the top of the puppet will be. Put the harder, grasping piece of velcro on the card. The softer, looped piece of velcro should go on the back of the puppet's head. For displaying each puppet in the classroom after its lesson day, string a line onto which you can clip the background cards or display them along the wall with tape.

Puppet Patterns

Each letter is accompanied by a puppet pattern. All patterns are shown actual size for finger puppets. For hand puppets use an opaque projector or a copy machine to enlarge patterns three times the finger puppet size. The basic body for each puppet is the same. Refer to the Finger Puppet Pattern section on page 8. The patterns for individualizing each puppet are included on the individual pattern pages.

How To Use *Whole Language Units for the Alphabet* *(cont.)*

Finger Puppet Pattern

The following is a list of supplies needed to make the puppets for the entire alphabet. Refer to the individual patterns for information concerning which colors to use for each puppet.

Supplies

felt:

dark brown	black	light green	dark green
orange	tan	gray	dark gray
red	lavender	dark pink	light pink
light blue	peach	white	yellow

52 wiggly eyes (Every puppet uses two wiggly eyes.)   black laundry pen

¼" (.6cm) pompom balls: 3 brown, 4 pink, 1 white, 5 black, 1 yellow

pipe cleaners: gray, pink, brown, black, red   scissors   glue

hot glue gun   needle   thread (assorted colors)

Basic Body Pattern

Directions:

1. For each puppet cut two pieces (front and back) using the Basic Body Pattern.

2. Glue or stitch the edges of the two pieces together leaving open the straight bottom section.

3. Do not turn inside out. Now it is ready for individualizing features. Turn to each letter for individualizing patterns.

Apples and Aunt Annie Ant

Albert Ant and Angela Ant waited for Aunt Annie Ant to come to their anthill.

Aunt Annie Ant brought apples for Albert Ant and Angela Ant.

"Apples, apples, apples. Who wants an apple?" asked Aunt Annie Ant.

"We do. We do," said Albert Ant and Angela Ant.

Albert Ant and Angela Ant ate apples.

Aunt Annie Ant told Albert Ant and Angela Ant a story.

Albert Ant and Angela Ant fell asleep by Aunt Annie Ant.

Using the Letter "Aa"

Word Bank

achieve	ache	act	add	adjust
aim	announce	annoy	appear	arrange
astonish	attach	alligator	author	assorted

Activities

1. Make an "ant" farm. Put soil into a clear glass jar. Add ants. Add several drops of water and food crumbs daily. Cover with nylons. Fasten securely. As much as possible, keep the ants in a dark place, because ants work the best in the dark. During the day, take the ant farm out of the dark for observation. For further observation, remove the nylon lid, place the jar in a shallow pan of water to prevent escapes, and lay a ruler across the top of the jar. The ants will come out of the jar and walk around on the ruler.

2. Learn about what to do in case there is an "accident" at home or at school. Talk about the emergency number 911.

3. Look at "advertisements" for children's items. Talk about the purpose of the advertisements. As a class make an advertisement for an event your class is planning.

4. Have an "All American Day." Wear red, white, and blue to school. Color the flag of the United States of America. Look at a picture of our country's American Eagle seal. Eat American cheese.

5. Study "apples." Estimate how many seeds are inside an apple. Cut the apple open to see whose guess was the closest. Dip the apple pieces into paint and use them for print painting. Examine different kinds of apples. Eat apples. Make and eat applesauce as follows. Pare apples (½ apple per child), place in large saucepan with one inch water. Cover and simmer until apples are tender. Process in blender if smoother sauce is desired.

Suggested Reading List

Allinson, Beverly. *Effie.* Scholastic Inc., 1990.

Brenner, Barbara. *You Were An Ant...* Harper & Row, 1973.

Davis, Arthur. *Ant Cities.* Harper & Row, 1987.

Hopf, Alice. *Biography of an Ant.* G.P. Putnam's Sons, 1974.

Van Allsburg, Chris. *Two Bad Ants.* Houghton Mifflin, 1988.

Name _____

Phonics Activity

Color the pictures that begin with the **A** sound.

Aa

Aunt Annie Ant

Ant Pattern

Colors: Black
Pink
Tan

Needs: Eyes

Basic Body: Tan
(See page 8 for directions.)

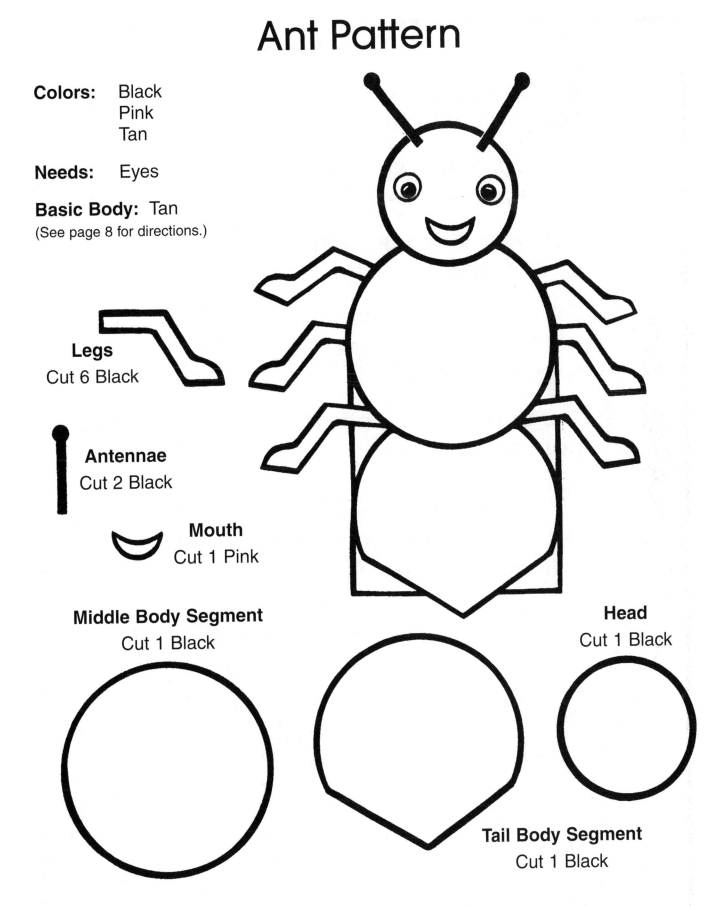

Legs
Cut 6 Black

Antennae
Cut 2 Black

Mouth
Cut 1 Pink

Middle Body Segment
Cut 1 Black

Head
Cut 1 Black

Tail Body Segment
Cut 1 Black

Glue legs to mid-body segment. Following the illustration glue all segments to the basic body. Add the remaining features as shown.

Bobby and The Big Brown Bear

Bobby saw a big brown bear with a beautiful blue bag.

The big brown bear blew into the beautiful blue bag.

The beautiful blue bag got bigger and bigger.

The big brown bear pulled a big balloon out of the beautiful blue bag.

The brown bear gave the big balloon to Bobby.

Bobby said, "Thank you."

Then the big brown bear blew away with his beautiful blue bag.

Using the Letter "Bb"

Word Bank

battle	behave	bicker	blow	bring
break	build	buy	buzz	bank
bat	banana	bird	beautiful	bright

Activities

1. Have a "Teddy Bear Day. " Have children bring their teddy bears. Sit on the rug and read bedtime or teddy bear stories. Have bear-shaped cookies and milk for a bedtime snack.

2. "Blow bubbles" with soapy water.

3. "Bake banana bread." Bake bread in individual muffin papers so each child will have a "loaf." Put butter on the banana bread. Increase this recipe according to the number of children in the class.

Banana Bread

2½ cups flour	½ cup brown sugar, packed
⅓ cup honey	3½ teaspoons baking powder
⅓ cup milk	1¼ cups mashed bananas
1 egg	2 tablespoons oil

Mix all ingredients together. Bake in greased 9" (23 cm) loaf pan at 350° F for 60 to 70 minutes. For muffin size loaves bake for 20 to 25 minutes. Makes about 10 to 12 muffins.

4. Make "bean bags" using old socks. Fill the toe with beans, then securely tie the open end of the sock. Play a relay game using the bean bags or use masking tape to make a giant tic-tac-toe board on the floor. Use the bean bags as markers for the game.

5. Have a "Backwards Day." Wear clothing backwards to school. Walk down the hall backwards. Eat dessert first at lunch. Be creative. Do other things backwards that are special to your class.

Suggested Reading List

Ainsworth, Ruth. *Goldilocks and the Three Bears.* Banner, 1979.

Bond, Michael. *Paddington Bear.* Random House, 1972.

Carlstrom, Nancy White. *Jesse Bear, What Will You Wear?* Macmillan, 1986.

Freeman, Don. *Corduroy.* The Viking Press, 1968.

Hoff, Syd. *Grizzwold.* Harper & Row, 1963.

Name _____

Phonics Activity

Color the pictures that begin with the **B** sound.

Bb

Big Brown Bear

Bear Pattern

Colors: Brown
Peach
Red

Needs: 2 Brown Pompoms
Eyes

Basic Body: Dark Brown
(See page 8 for directions.)

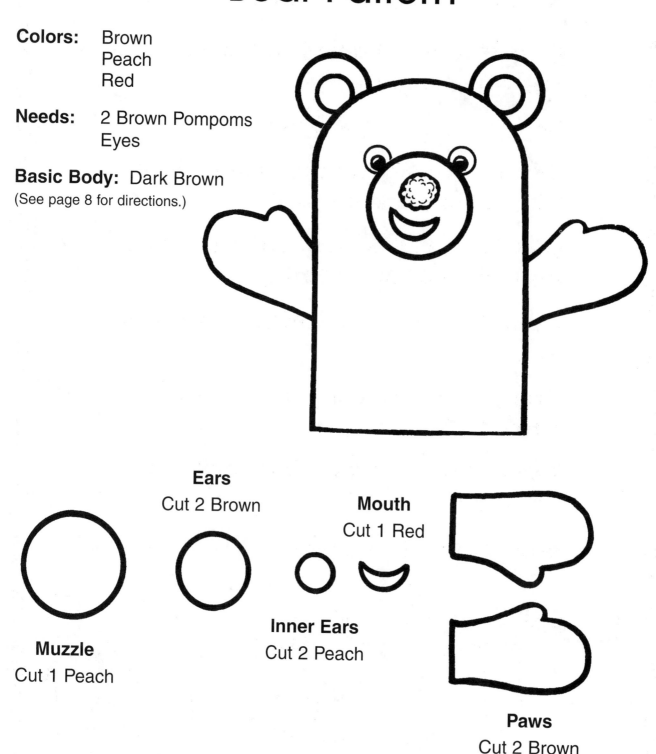

Ears
Cut 2 Brown

Mouth
Cut 1 Red

Muzzle
Cut 1 Peach

Inner Ears
Cut 2 Peach

Paws
Cut 2 Brown

Place peach circles on centers of brown circles and sandwich between body halves for ears. Sandwich paws with thumbs up. Glue one pompom and one mouth to muzzle, glue muzzle to body, and glue one pompom to lower back for tail. Attach eyes.

Cat Food For Cami Cat

Cami Cat crept across the carpet. She was hungry.

Up the curtains she went.

Cami Cat tried to catch the cuckoo bird in the cuckoo clock.

Silly Cami Cat cannot eat a cuckoo bird! She eats cat food.

Cami Cat climbed down the curtains to her cat dish.

"Yum, yum. Cat food is good," said Cami Cat.

Cami Cat was tired after eating her cat food.

She curled up on the couch for a catnap.

Using the Letter "Cc"

Word Bank

cackle	camp	cut	carry	clean
cling	close	color	comb	control
cook	cry	calculator	candle	carpet

Activities

1. Get large refrigerator, dishwasher, and range boxes from an appliance store. Cut the boxes into castle shapes. Let the children decorate the "castles."

2. Discuss having "colds." Remind children to cover their mouths when they cough or sneeze! Cut large ovals for children to use for drawing their faces. After having the children draw their faces on the oval, trace each child's hand and part of the arm. Cut out the hands. Glue a tissue over the mouth on each child's face drawing and then glue the hand over the tissue to emphasize covering the mouth during coughing or sneezing.

3. Have a "Clown Day." Children should come to school dressed as clowns or decorate large grocery bags to wear. Cut holes for arms and head. Paint faces with inexpensive grease paints that can be purchased in a novelty store or department store. Cut out a large clown figure and play Pin the Nose on the Clown. Play the game using the same format as Pin the Tail on the Donkey.

4. Play "carnival" games such as ring toss, rolling the ball to knock down bottles (blocks), and breaking balloons by sitting on them.

5. Make "crystal" snowstorms. You will need 9" x 12" (23cm x 30cm) blue construction paper, crystal glitter, winter pictures cut from magazines, glue, water, and paintbrushes. Glue the magazine pictures to the blue construction paper. Water the glue down. Brush the solution over the entire sheet. Sprinkle with crystal glitter. Shake off excess. Let the pictures dry again and shake off excess glitter. (To update — use glitter glue & a paintbrush — no glitter mess!)

Suggested Reading List

Averill, Esther. *The Fire Cat.* Harper & Row, 1960.

Freschet, Bernice. *Furlie Cat.* Lothrop, Lee & Shepard, 1986.

Knotts, Howard. *The Summer Cat.* Harper & Row, 1981.

McPhail, David. *Great Cat.* E.P. Dutton, 1982.

Seuss, Dr. *The Cat in the Hat.* Random House, 1957.

Phonics Activity

Color the pictures that begin with the **C** sound.

Cc

Cami Cat

Cat Pattern

Colors: Black
              White
              Dark Gray
              Pink
              Red

Needs: Thread for Whiskers
              Eyes

Basic Body: Black

(See page 8 for directions.)

Paws
Cut 2 Dark Gray

Nose
Cut 1 Pink

Tongue
Cut 1 Red

Ears
Cut 2 Black

Muzzle
Cut 1 White

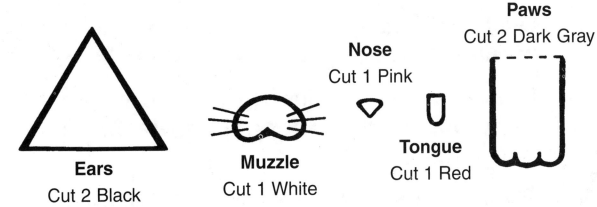

Tail
Cut 1 Dark Gray

Glue tongue behind muzzle, and glue nose onto muzzle. Sandwich ears between body halves. Add tail to lower back. Glue eyes, paws, and whiskers as shown.

Donald's Dogs and the Doughnuts

Donald's dogs were named Dusty and Dapper.

Dusty and Dapper liked to eat doughnuts with Donald.

Donald gave Dusty and Dapper dinner.

"What?" barked Dusty and Dapper. "This is just dog food."

Dusty and Dapper barked. "Doughnuts, doughnuts, doughnuts!"

Donald came running. "Do not bark, Dusty and Dapper. Eat your dog food."

Dusty and Dapper barked again. "Doughnuts, doughnuts, doughnuts!"

Donald came running again. "Do not bark, Dusty and Dapper. Here are some doughnuts!"

Then Dusty and Dapper were happy. They ate all the doughnuts.

Using the Letter "Dd"

Word Bank

dash	dazzle	deal	defend	devour
disappear	disapprove	dislike	dodge	drag
draw	dump	degree	dessert	double

Activities

1. Make a "dog bone necklace." You will need bone-shaped dog treats, yarn cut to appropriate lengths to make necklaces and markers, glitter or other decorating material. Tie the dog bone in the middle with the yarn. Decorate and wear.

2. For art time make a "dog." Use a toilet paper roll for the body. Paint or glue cotton to it. Use a 1" (2.54 cm) pompom for the head and a ¼" (.6 cm) pompom for the nose. Add wiggly eyes, felt ears, and legs and tail out of pipe cleaners.

3. Have each child bring a "doll" or stuffed animal. Discuss and discover how the dolls or animals are dressed, and what they can do. Decide which doll or animal is distinctive, deluxe, dramatic, difficult, different, delicate, detailed, or dear.

4. Study "dinosaurs." Read books about dinosaurs. Study the pictures and names of some dinosaurs. Make a large stuffed dinosaur using butcher paper. Draw the outline of your chosen dinosaur onto a 12 foot (3.6 m) length of butcher paper that is doubled to form a 6 foot (1.8 m) length. Following your outline, cut through both thicknesses of the paper. Staple the sides of the dinosaur, stuffing it with wadded newspaper as you staple. Include the children in as much of the construction as possible. When the dinosaur is stuffed and stapled, have the children paint it. You may want to make more than one to accommodate the number of children in your class.

5. Make a "drum." Use empty oatmeal boxes or tin cans for the drum bodies. Cover the open ends with fabric or a plastic lid. Attach with glue or a rubber band. Decorate the body of the drum with pictures or with paint.

Suggested Reading List

Bridwell, Norman. *Clifford's Birthday Party.* Scholastic Inc., 1988.

Cuyler, Margery. *Freckles and Jane.* Henry Holt and Company, 1989.

Frith, Michael. *I'll Teach My Dog 100 Words.* Random House, Inc., 1973.

Gackenback, Dick. *Pepper and All the Legs.* Clarion Books, 1978.

Havill, Juanita. *Jamaica's Find.* Houghton Mifflin, 1986.

Name _____

Phonics Activity

Color the pictures that begin with the **D** sound.

Dd

Dusty and Dapper Dog

Dog Pattern

Colors: Gray
Dark Gray
Black
Red

Needs: One Black Popcorn
Eyes

Basic Body: Gray
(See page 8 for directions.)

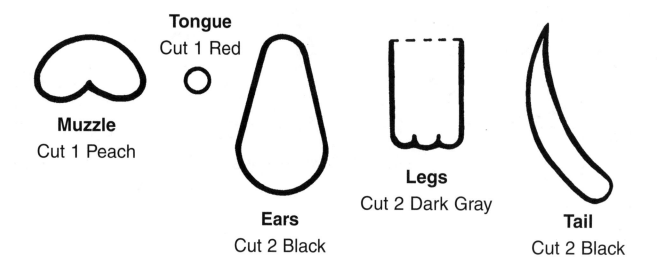

Tongue
Cut 1 Red

Muzzle
Cut 1 Peach

Ears
Cut 2 Black

Legs
Cut 2 Dark Gray

Tail
Cut 2 Black

Glue tongue behind muzzle. Attach pompom onto muzzle. Attach tail to back of puppet. Glue other parts as shown.

The Enormous Ears

Everett Elephant had enormous ears.

Edgar Elephant had enormous ears.

"My ears are the most enormous," said Everett Elephant.

"My ears are the most enormous," said Edgar Elephant.

"I will decide," said Edward Elephant.

Edward Elephant measured Everett Elephant's ears.

Edward Elephant measured Edgar Elephant's ears.

"Everett Elephant and Edgar Elephant's ears are the same size," said Edward Elephant.

Everett Elephant and Edgar Elephant both have enormous ears.

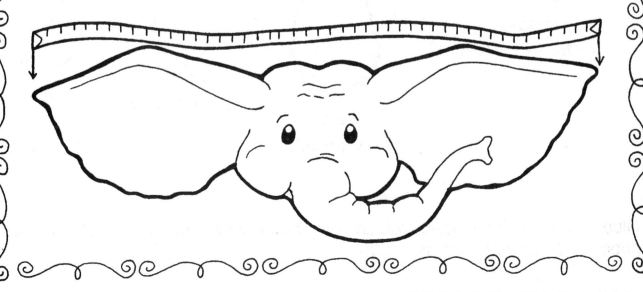

 #202 Early Childhood Units for the Alphabet

Using the Letter "Ee"

Word Bank

eat	enlarge	enter	escape	exaggerate
examine	excite	exit	explain	experiment
earth	easel	ecology	elementary	endangered

Activities

1. Have children pretend to be "elephants." With arms straight out, clasp hands together in front. Raise arms up high and make trumpeting sounds. Lower arms and swing them back and forth in front of body.

2. Listen to "echoes." Do this in an empty room or hallway. Use a wrapping paper or paper towel tube. Have one child speak into an end of the tube. Another child can hear the echo by listening on the other end of the tube.

3. Paint or draw different color E's on "envelopes." Collect E's from newspapers and magazines to put in the envelopes.

4. Although it may not be Easter, coloring "eggs" is fun to do anytime. Inexpensive dye may be made by adding 1 tablespoon vinegar and several drops of food coloring to a cup of hot water. To avoid burns, let the water cool somewhat before allowing the children to dip hard-boiled eggs into it. For designs on the eggs, have the children draw on the eggs with crayons before dipping.

5. Introduce children to the concept of "estimation" by filling a jar with candy. Allow each child to estimate (guess) how many pieces of candy are in the jar. Guide the guesses so they are somewhat realistic. When each child has had a chance to estimate, count the candy to see who had the closest estimate. Share a piece of candy with each child when you are finished.

Suggested Reading List

Caple, Kathy. *The Biggest Nose.* Houghton Mifflin, 1985.

Hall, Derek. *Elephant Bathes.* Alfred A. Knopf, 1985.

Hoff Syd. *Oliver.* Harper & Row, 1960.

Lobel, Arnold. *Uncle Elephant.* Harper & Row, 1981.

Peet, Bill. *Encore for Eleanor.* Houghton Mifflin, 1981.

Name _____

Phonics Activity

Color the pictures that begin with the **E** sound.

Ee

Everett Elephant

Elephant Pattern

Colors: Gray
White

Needs: Eyes

Basic Body: Gray
(See page 8 for directions.)

Head and Trunk
Cut 1 Gray

Ears
Cut 2 Gray

Feet
Cut 2 Gray

Tail
Cut 1 Gray

Tusks
Cut 2 White

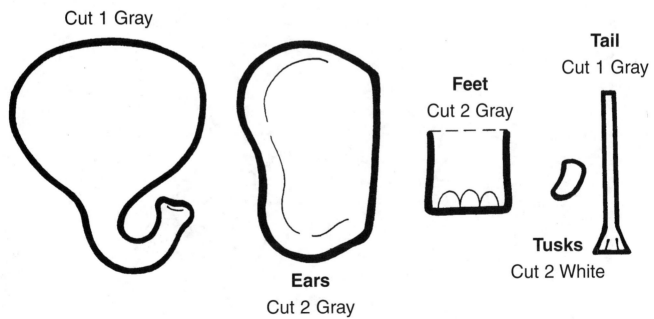

Glue the tail, trunk, tusks, eyes and ears as shown.

Flo Frog Fell

Frank Frog fixed four logs.

Flo Frog hopped onto the logs.

She fell into the water.

Frank Frog hopped into the water to help Flo Frog.

He helped Flo Frog out of the water.

Frank Frog helped Flo Frog sit on the four logs.

Frank Frog fed Flo Frog five flies.

Flo Frog was fine!

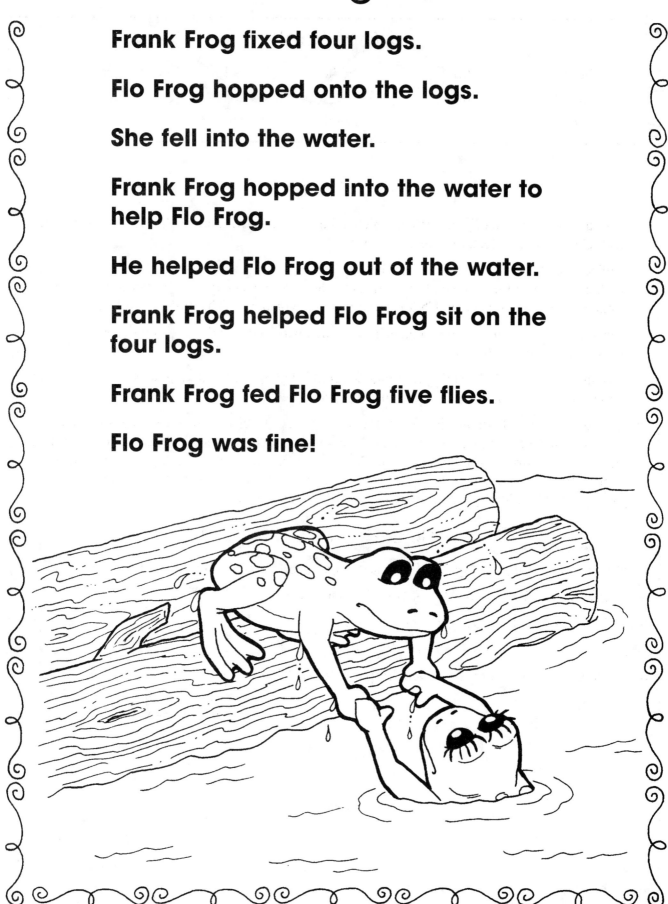

Using the Letter "Ff"

Word Bank

feel	fib	fiddle	fight	figure
find	float	follow	frighten	fuss
fashion	feast	flood	fancy	false

Activities

1. Talk about animal "feet." Determine which animals have hooves, cloven hooves, paws, webbed feet, claws, toes, no feet, two feet, or four feet.

2. Collect "feathers" for the children to feel. Keep them in boxes or plastic bags. Have the children look at and touch the feathers. Use pictures to show from which type of bird each feather came. This can be done as a center. Children can match the pictures of the birds to the feathers.

3. Make a "fantastic fan" for warm days. Use a small paper plate and a craft stick. Decorate the plate. Glue it to the stick.

4. Discuss "families." Each child has a unique family. Talk about family members. If possible, talk about the students' families to make the discussion more personal.

5. Set up a "fish pond" in the classroom. Put small prizes (pencils, erasers, toys, etc.) into a box or basket. Make a fishing pole with a hook. The hook is made by opening a paper clip and tying to the end of the string. If the prizes do not have natural places on them for hooking, tie string around them so they can be easily "caught." When a child has accomplished something in the class reward him/her by letting him/her "go fish" in the pond.

Suggested Reading List

Dauer, Rosemond. *Bullfrog and Gertrude Go Camping.* Greenwillow Books, 1980.

Duke, Kate. *Seven Froggies Went to School.* E.P. Dutton, 1985.

Kalan, Robert. *Jump, Frog, Jump!* Scholastic Inc., 1981.

Langstaff, John. *Frog Went A-Courtin'.* HBJ, 1955.

Lobel, Arnold. *Frog and Toad Together.* Harper & Row, 1971, 1972.

Phonics Activity

Color the pictures that begin with the **F** sound.

Ff

Frank and Flo Frog

Frog Pattern

Colors: Dark Green
Light Green
White

Needs: Eyes
1" (2.54 cm) red pipe cleaner

Basic Body: Dark Green
(See page 8 for directions.)

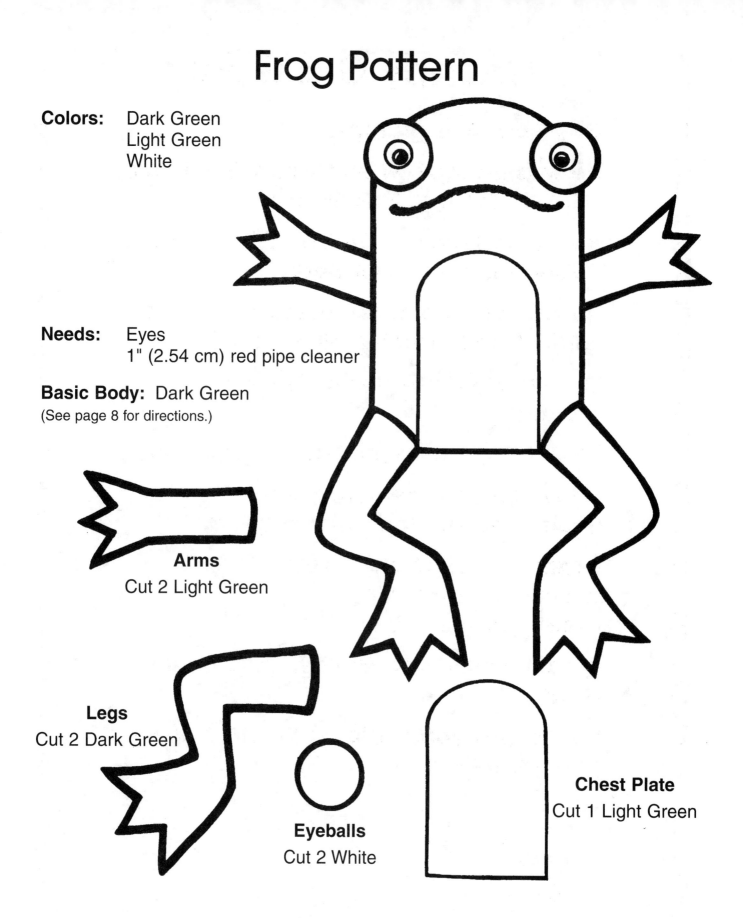

Arms
Cut 2 Light Green

Legs
Cut 2 Dark Green

Eyeballs
Cut 2 White

Chest Plate
Cut 1 Light Green

Glue the legs and eyeballs as shown in the illustration. Center the wiggly eyes inside the eyeballs and glue. Bend the 1" (2.54 cm) red pipe cleaner and glue, centered under the eyeballs with the sides of the mouth pointing as shown.

Grumpy Gus Goat

Gus Goat was grumpy.

He was grumpy when Granny Goat said, "Good morning, Gus Goat."

He was grumpy when Greta Goose said, "Good morning, Gus Goat."

He was grumpy when Greta's goslings said, "Good morning, Gus Goat."

Granny Goat knew why Gus was grumpy.

"Gus Goat is hungry," said Granny Goat.

"Have some green grapes with us," said Greta Goose, "You will feel great."

Granny Goat, Greta Goose, Greta's goslings and grumpy Gus Goat ate green grapes.

"Thank you, Greta Goose," said Granny Goat.

"Oh, thank you," said Gus Goat. "Now I feel great!"

Using the Letter "Gg"

Word Bank

gargle	giggle	gobble	grip	groan
grow	grumble	guess	guide	goat
grapes	grass	garden	grandparent	grumpy

Activities

1. Have a "Great Green Day" at school. Wear something green to school. Write only with a green crayon or marker.

2. Have a "Glove Day." Play relay games in which children unwrap candy, eat grapes, and pick up game pieces with gloves on their hands. Practice right and left using gloves. Children should put on the right glove when the teacher says "right" and the left glove when the teacher says "left."

3. "Grow green grass." Use small plastic-lined baskets or milk jugs that have been cut to about 2" (5 cm) in height. Cover the bottom of the container to about 1½" (4 cm) with dirt or potting soil. Sprinkle grass seed over the dirt or soil. Pat down to cover seeds. Water gently. Be sure the seeds get enough water and light to grow. The grass will grow several inches high.

4. Have a "Grandparents's Day." Invite grandparents or someone special to school for a day or a portion of a day. Each grandparent should bring something that begins with or in some way ties in with the letter G. If grandparents cannot come in person, students could bring pictures of them.

5. Using cellophane Easter "grass" make a picture on construction paper. You will need 9" x 12" (23 cm x 30 cm) white, brown, and green construction paper, green Easter grass, small green, pink, and yellow tissue paper squares, scissors, and glue. Have children glue the grass to the bottom of the white paper. Make trees from the brown and green paper. Glue them onto the grass. Use tissue paper squares to make leaves or flowers growing up from the grass.

Suggested Reading List

Gregorich, Barbara. *Up Went the Goat.* School Zone, 1984.

Milios, Rita. *The Hungry Billy Goat.* Childrens Press, 1989.

Pizer, Abigail. *Hattie the Goat.* Carolrhoda Books, Inc., 1989.

Rockwell, Ann. *Big Bad Goat.* E.P. Dutton, 1982.

Sharmat, Mitchell. *Gregory, The Terrible Eater.* Scholastic, 1980.

Phonics Activity

Color the pictures that begin with the **G** sound.

Gg

Grumpy Gus Goat

Goat Pattern

Colors: White
Gray
Black
Tan

Needs: Eyes

Basic Body: Black
(See page 8 for directions.)

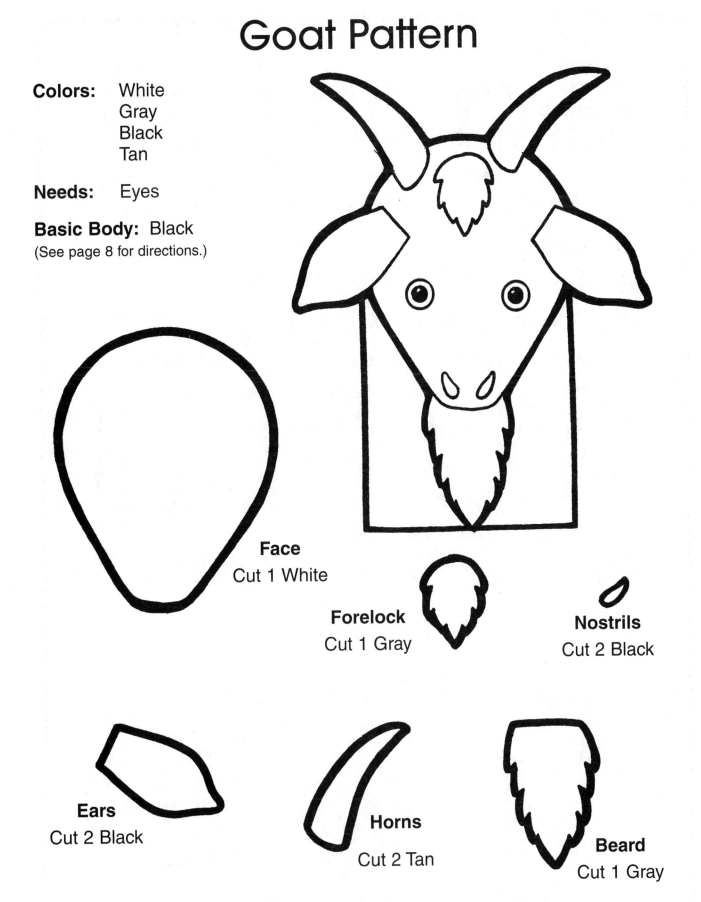

Face
Cut 1 White

Forelock
Cut 1 Gray

Nostrils
Cut 2 Black

Ears
Cut 2 Black

Horns
Cut 2 Tan

Beard
Cut 1 Gray

Glue features into place following illustration.

Hanna Hen's Hay-filled Nest

Hanna Hen has her house on a hill.

Hanna's hay-filled nest is in the house.

Hanna Hen sits on her hay-filled nest. What is under Hanna Hen?

Under Hanna Hen are ten eggs. She sits on them to keep them hot.

"Peep, peep, peep."

Hanna Hen now has chicks in her hay-filled nest in her house on the hill.

Hooray for Hanna Hen! Hooray! Hooray!

Hooray for the ten chicks in Hanna Hen's hay-filled nest!

Using the Letter "Hh"

Word Bank

handle	hang	hate	herd	hiccup
heave	hum	hug	hurt	habit
hammer	hearing	hurricane	handsome	harvest

Activities

1. Help the children in your class learn about "handicaps." Spend a day discussing different kinds of handicaps and how to treat handicapped people. Put socks on the children's hands and ask them to color a picture or pick up small toys. Put a blindfold on children and let them feel their way around the room. These are ways to help children begin to empathize with handicapped people. Be sure to discuss all experiences.

2. Look in magazines to find pictures of "happy" people. Cut out the pictures, glue them onto a large piece of butcher paper to make a large happy mural. Discuss things that make the children in your class happy. Write those things on the mural, too.

3. Have a "Hat Day." Ask all the children to wear a hat on their heads when they come to school. Look for similarities and differences between hats. Look for high, huge, and hunting hats.

4. Talk about different types of "homes." Some people live in houses, some live in apartments, some live in trailers, some in nursing homes. Have each child illustrate his/her home. Talk about Hanna Hen's home and incubating eggs.

5. Help the children outline their "hands" on construction paper. Cut out the hands and hang them on a bulletin board in the shape of an H.

Suggested Reading List

Dodds, Siobhan. *Elizabeth Hen.* Little, Brown and Company, 1987.

Domanska, Janina. *Little Red Hen.* Macmillan, 1973.

Freschet, Bernice. *Where's Henrietta's Hen?* G.P. Putnam's Sons, 1980.

Galdone, Paul. *Henny Penny.* Houghton Mifflin, 1968.

Polushkin, Maria. *The Little Hen and the Giant.* Harper & Row, 1977.

Name _____

Phonics Activity

Color the pictures that begin with the **H** sound.

Hh

Hanna Hen

Hen Pattern

Colors: Red
Orange
Yellow
White

Needs: Eyes

Basic Body: Tan
(See page 8 for directions.)

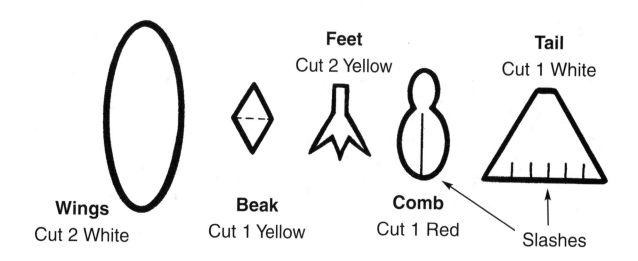

Wings
Cut 2 White

Beak
Cut 1 Yellow

Feet
Cut 2 Yellow

Comb
Cut 1 Red

Tail
Cut 1 White

Slashes

Glue wings, eyes, and feet as shown in illustration. Glue tail to lower back. Glue the slash of the comb to the top of the head so that one part of the slash is in the front and the other part in the back. Fold the beak and glue in the crease so that the beak will stay folded, but not so it is glued completely shut. Glue into place.

We Want To Ice Skate

Ingrid Insect invited Inky Inchworm to ice skate.

"I am ill," said Inky Inchworm. "I will skate when I am well."

Ingrid Insect was sorry Inky Inchworm was ill.

"I will make Inky Inchworm a surprise," she said.

Ingrid worked very hard.

Ingrid took the surprise to Inky.

"Here is a surprise for you, Inky Inchworm, because you are ill," said Ingrid Insect.

Inky's surprise was a new ice skate!

"Thank you," said Inky. "Now I am not ill. I want to ice skate."

"Wow," said Ingrid. "We will go now!"

Using the Letter "Ii"

Word Bank

ignore	illustrate	imagine	improve	inflate
inform	injure	investigate	invite	irrigate
itch	illness	infant	impatient	incomplete

Activities

1. Use sugar cubes to make an "igloo." Using glue, fasten sugar cubes together to form an igloo or use cotton glued to a small margarine container. Sprinkle the cotton with clear glitter to look like ice.

2. Have the children bring "insects" to school for sharing. If alive, the insects should be in jars with the lids tightly closed. Small holes can be poked in the lids for air. Discuss the insects inhaling the air. Discuss differences in insects.

3. Assign several children to "inspect" the classroom before it is time to go home. Have them see if all the paper is off the floor and the toys and books are put away in the right places.

4. Make "invisible ink" pictures. Draw the pictures in lemon juice. To see the picture, heat the picture over a light bulb. The writing will turn brown.

5. Since a butterfly is a type of insect, have children make butterflies from construction paper and tissue. You will need 9" x 12" (23cm x 30cm) light colored construction paper, colored tissue squares, pipe cleaners, scissors, and glue.
   Duplicate the pattern of a butterfly (page 51) onto the construction paper. Have the children glue 2" (5cm) squares of colored tissue paper to the butterfly's wings. Glue the pipe cleaners into place for the antennae.

Suggested Reading List

Milne, Lorus and Margery. *The Audubon Society Field Guide to North American Insects and Spiders.* Alfred A. Knopf, 1980.

Mound, Laurence. *Eyewitness Books Insect.* Alfred A. Knopf, 1990.

O'Toole, Christopher. *Insects and Spiders.* New York: Facts on File, 1990.

Sonza, D.M. *Insects in the Garden.* Carolrhoda Books, 1991.

Wexo, John Bonnett. *Insects.* Creative Education, Inc., 1989.

Butterfly Pattern

Name _____

Phonics Activity

Color the pictures that begin with the **I** sound.

Ii

Ingrid Insect and Inky Inchworm

Insect Pattern

Colors: Dark Green
Light Green
Brown
Lavender
Red

Needs: Two Black 1" (2.54 cm) pipe cleaners
Eyes

Basic Body: Dark Green
(See page 8 for directions.)

Wings/Chest Plate
Cut 2 Lavender for Wings
Cut 1 Light Green for Chest Plate

Head
Cut 1 Light Green

Legs
Cut 6 Brown

Mouth
Cut 1 Red

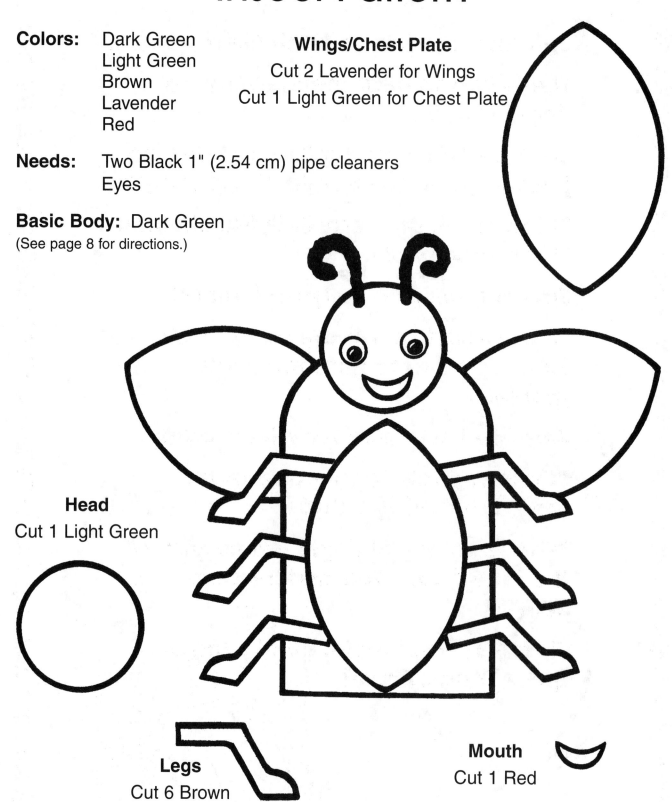

Glue the head to the top of the basic body. Space the legs evenly and sandwich between chest plate and body. Glue the wings centered and touching at the points so that they come about even with the bottom of the body. Curl pipe cleaners and glue to head. Glue eyes and mouth into place.

Jingle Jangle

Jan and Jessica Jellyfish liked jewelry.

They liked to hear their jewelry go jingle jangle.

Jerry Jellyfish did not like to hear the jewelry go jingle jangle, jingle jangle.

"Stop jingling!" Jerry Jellyfish shouted. "Stop jangling!"

Jan and Jessica Jellyfish jumped.

"Jerry Jellyfish, we are sorry," they said. "We like to hear the jingle jangle."

Jerry Jellyfish was sorry he shouted.

"Please, jingle jangle part of the time," said Jerry Jellyfish.

"Our jewelry will jingle jangle part of the time," said Jan and Jessica Jellyfish.

Jingle, quiet, jangle, quiet. Jingle, quiet, jangle, quiet.

Using the Letter "J j"

Word Bank

jeer	jest	jiggle	jingle	jog
joke	jolt	judge	juggle	jump
jazz	jasmine	jungle	jolly	juicy

Activities

1. Attach "jingle bells" to small pieces of felt. Use the jingle bells for practicing different patterns of jingling. Have a jingle bell band.

2. Teach the children how to "juggle. " Use handkerchiefs or bandannas. Very lightweight nylon scarves work well. Begin by throwing one scarf into the air. Smaller children will have an easier time learning to juggle only two scarves. Later, if they are able, add another scarf to juggle three at a time.

3. Take a "trip" to the "jungle. " Roar like a lion. Slither like a snake. Chirp like a bird. Eat bananas and coconuts. Hang green and brown crepe paper from the ceiling for jungle vegetation.

4. Locate the country of "Japan" on a map. Discuss customs of the Japanese people. Look at pictures of their traditional dress. Eat rice with chopsticks. Make Japanese fans. Cut a 6" x 9" (15 cm x 23 cm) piece of construction paper. Fanfold the paper beginning on a 6" (15 cm) side. When the entire paper is fan folded, use a paper clip on one end to hold the fan together or staple.

5. Have a "Junk Day." Go outside to the playground or the neighborhood to pick up junk (litter). Discuss putting junk where it belongs, recycling, and reusing items.

Suggested Reading List

Coldrey, Jennifer. *Jellyfish and Other Sea Creatures.* Oxford Scientific Films, G.P. Putnam's Sons, 1981.

MacQuity, Miranda. *Discovery Jellyfish.* The Bookwright Press, 1989.

Menkoth, Norman A. *The Audubon Society Field Guide to North American Seashore Creatures.* Alfred A. Knopf, 1989.

Podendorf, Illa. *Animals of Sea and Shore.* Regensteiner Enterprises, 1982.

Shale, David and Jennifer Coldrey. *The World of Jellyfish.* Gareth Stevens Publishing, 1987.

Name _____

Phonics Activity

Color the pictures that begin with the **J** sound.

Jj

Jan, Jessica, & Jerry Jellyfish

Jellyfish Pattern

Colors: Light Pink
              Dark Pink
              Lavender

Needs: Eyes

Basic Body: Light Pink
(See page 8 for directions.)

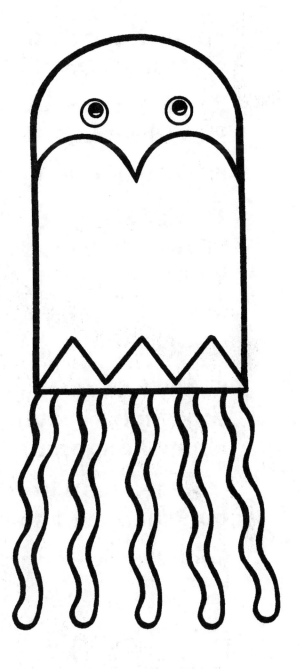

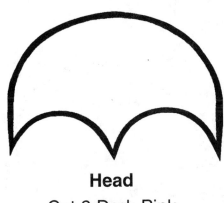

Head
Cut 2 Dark Pink

Body Decoration
Cut 2 Lavender

Cut ten ⅛" x 3" (.3 cm x 8 cm) strips of dark pink felt for trailing tentacles. Glue the tentacles to the bottom of the basic body—5 to each side. (Yarn, ribbon, or paper strips can also be used as tentacles.) Glue the body decoration over where the tentacles are glued to the body (one on each side). Glue one head to each side of the top of the body. Glue the eyes to the head as shown in the illustration.

Ketchup For Kenny Kangaroo

Kenny Kangaroo was asleep in his mother's pocket.

Kenny Kangaroo kinked his tail and kicked his feet.

"I am hungry," said Kenny Kangaroo.

Mother Kangaroo hopped to the kitchen. She made ketchup in a kettle.

Kenny Kangaroo ate ketchup on his sandwich.

Kenny Kangaroo ate all the sandwich. "Excuse me, please," said Kenny Kangaroo.

Mother kissed Kenny Kangaroo and put him back into her pocket.

Soon Kenny Kangaroo was asleep.

Ketchup For Kenny Kangaroo

Using the Letter "Kk"

Word Bank

keep	kick	kid	kindle	kink
kiss	katydid	karate	keyboard	king
kite	kayak	kingdom	keen	kind

Activities

1. Make a "kangaroo" pocket in which to keep special items. Kangaroos keep babies in their pockets. Discuss what the children might keep in theirs. You will need 9" x 12" (23 cm x 30 cm) construction paper, glue, and decorating supplies. Fold a piece of construction paper in half. The 9" (23 cm) ends will face each other. Glue the sides. Decorate.

2. Draw the outline of a large "key." Duplicate the key onto white construction paper so it can be colored. Punch a hole near the top of the key. String yarn through it for a necklace.

3. Celebrate "kids!" Have each child bring a picture of himself/herself to school along with a special toy or book to share with the class. Let the kids choose a special game or activity. Let the children know that kids are special.

4. Make "kites." You will need 12" x 18" (30 cm x 46 cm) construction paper, cotton-tipped swabs, paint, and yarn. Cut a diamond shape from a 12" x 18" (30 cm x 46 cm) piece of construction paper. Decorate by dipping the cotton-tipped swab into paint and using it for a paint brush. When dry, attach yarn for the kite tail.

5. Look at a Japanese "kimono." Make your own kimono by folding a sheet in half, cutting a hole for the head and tying a sash of fabric or a scarf around the waist.

Suggested Reading List

Burt, Denise and Neil McLeod. **Kangaroos.** Houghton Mifflin, 1989.

Cole, Joanna. **Norma Jean**, **Jumping Bean.** Random House, 1987.

Hurd, Edith Thacher. **The Mother Kangaroo.** Little, Brown and Company, 1976.

Payne, Emmy. **Katy No-Pocket.** Houghton Mifflin Company, 1944.

Petty, Kate. **Baby Animals Kangaroos.** Gloucester Press, 1990.

Name _____

Phonics Activity

Color the pictures that begin with the **K** sound.

Kk

Kenny Kangaroo

Kangaroo Pattern

Colors: Brown
Tan

Needs: 1 Pink Pompom
Eyes

Basic Body: Brown
(See page 8 for directions.)

Arms

Cut 1 Each Brown

Ears

Cut 2 Tan

Muzzle

Cut 1 Tan

Baby Kangaroo

Cut 1 Tan

Pocket

Cut 1 Brown

Tail

Cut 1 Brown

Glue mother's arms at about the middle of the body with enough space so that the baby kangaroo will fit between them. Glue the baby to the mother's body near the hands of the arms. Glue the pocket over the baby as shown. Glue eyes, ears, muzzle, and pompom nose into place. Draw mouth. Glue the tail pointing upward centered near the bottom back of the basic body.

Lemon Lollipops

Little Lenny Lion licked a large lemon lollipop.

Little Lenny Lion laughed loudly.

Little Linda Lion looked around a log.

"May I lick a large lemon lollipop, too?" she asked loudly.

"I love licking large lemon lollipops," said little Linda Lion.

"Here is a large lemon lollipop for you, little Linda Lion," said little Lenny Lion.

The little lions licked and licked the large lemon lollipops.

Soon the large lemon lollipops were little lemon lollipops!

Using the Letter "Ll"

Word Bank

lag	laugh	lean	learn	leave
lend	landscape	look	loose	lady
lick	litter	lacy	latest	liquid

Activities

1. Roar like a "lion. " Roar softly and then roar loudly. Roar while on all fours like a lion. Lumber around like a lion.

2. Make "Little Lenny Lion" faces from paper plates. You will need 9" (23 cm) paper plates, paint, brushes or yarn scissors, construction paper, glue, and a lollipop. Have the children paint the paper plates yellow or leave white and use yellow yarn for the mane. Cut slits around the plate about 1½" (3.84 cm) deep for the mane. Add construction paper eyes, ears, nose, mouth, and tongue. Glue a lollipop near the mouth. Think of a name for your lion that starts with L.

3. Do "lettuce leaf" painting. Put some paint on a sponge, press the lettuce leaf onto the sponge, and then press it onto a piece of paper.

4. Cut L's out of sticky-back "labels" and let the children put L's on their left hands. Practice recognizing left and right. Wiggle the left hand. Wiggle the right hand. Wiggle legs, toes, ears, and eyes.

5. "Lick lollipops" while listening to lullabies. Sing some of the lullabies.

Suggested Reading List

Allen, Pamela. *A Lion in the Night.* G.P. Putnam's Sons, 1985.

Fatio, Louise. *The Happy Lion Roars.* McGraw-Hill, 1957.

Fields, Julia. *The Green Lion of Zion Street.* Macmillan, 1988.

Hurd, Edith Thacher. *Johnny Lion's Book.* Harper & Row, 1965.

Peet, Bill. *Randy's Dandy Lions.* Houghton Mifflin, 1964.

Name _____

Phonics Activity

Color the pictures that begin with the **L** sound.

Ll

Little Lenny Lion

Lion Pattern

Colors: Tan
             Yellow
             Brown
             Red

Needs: Eyes
             Brown Pipe Cleaner
             Yellow Pompom

Basic Body: Tan
(See page 8 for directions.)

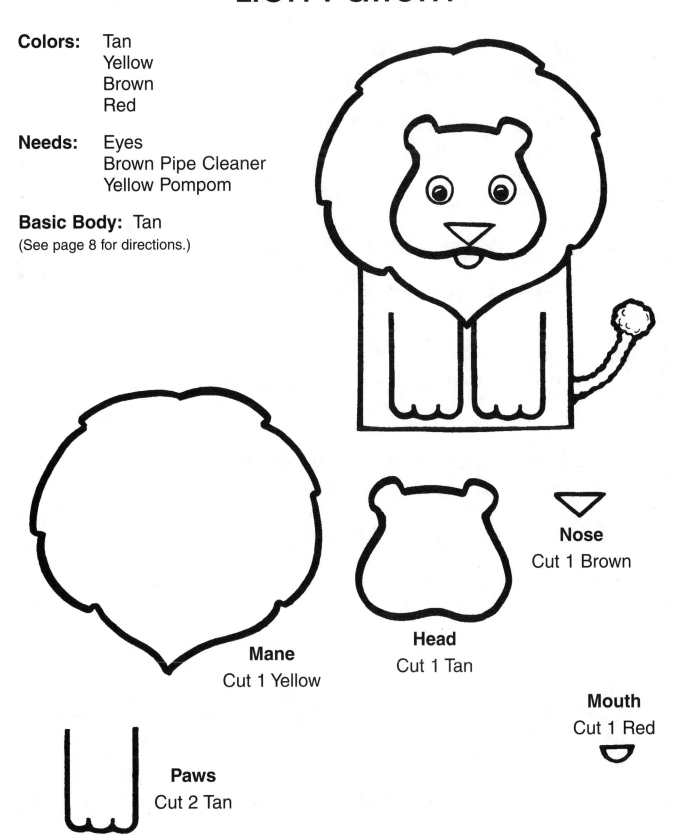

Mane
Cut 1 Yellow

Head
Cut 1 Tan

Nose
Cut 1 Brown

Mouth
Cut 1 Red

Paws
Cut 2 Tan

Glue the features to the basic body following the illustration.

Martin Mouse's Messy House

Martin Mouse had a mini house under a maple tree.

Mother Mouse was coming. What could Martin Mouse do?

Mud messed up the floor.

Mail messed up the table.

Mittens messed up the chairs.

Martin Mouse worked very hard.

When Mother Mouse came, the mess was gone!

Martin Mouse and Mother Mouse munched marshmallows and milk.

They did not make a mess!

Using the Letter "Mm"

Word Bank

mark	massage	match	maul	mend
mock	muffle	mumble	material	medicine
memory	mountain	motionless	magical	moist

Activities

1. Have a "Munchies Day." Each child should bring a snack that begins with M, such as marshmallows, marble cake, macaroni, macadamia nuts, macaroon cookies, maple syrup, or mandarin oranges.

2. Study "magnets." Make magnets by rubbing a nail or pin on a powerful magnet. Be sure to rub the nail in the same direction each time you stroke the magnet. See what the magnets will pick up. Find where the magnet is the strongest—is it in the middle or at the ends?

3. Use a "measuring stick" to measure things that start with M. For example, how long is a magic marker? How long is a McIntosh apple? How tall is a marshmallow?

4. Make a walnut "mouse." For each mouse you will need gray or white poster paint, one-half walnut shell, felt for nose, eyes and ears, and yarn for the tail. Paint the walnut shell gray or white. Cut ears, nose, and eyes from felt and glue into place on the pointed end of the shell. Glue a small piece of yarn to the underside of the rounded end of the shell for the tail.

5. Study and discuss the different phases of the "moon." Have children make the different phases. You will need large circles of white construction paper, paint, sponges, string, scissors and a stapler.

   Sponge paint both sides of the circle with yellow paint. The surface should look textured and uneven. Let dry. Staple the string to the moon and hang.

Suggested Reading List

Kraus, Robert. *Whose Mouse Are You?* Macmillan, 1970.

Kraus, Robert. *Another Mouse to Feed.* Simon and Schuster, 1980.

Lionni, Leo. *Alexander and the Wind-Up Mouse.* Alfred A. Knopf, 1969.

Miller, Moira and Maria Majewska. *Oscar Mouse Finds a Home.* Dial Books for Young Readers, 1985.

Numeroff, Laura Joffe. *If You Give a Mouse a Cookie.* Harper & Row, 1985.

Phonics Activity

Color the pictures that begin with the **M** sound.

72

Mm

Martin Mouse

 #202 Early Childhood Units for the Alphabet

Mouse Pattern

Colors: Gray
White
Pink

Needs: Gray Pipe Cleaner
Pink Pompom
6 Pink "hole punched" dots
Black Thread or Bristle for Whiskers
Red Thread, Fabric Paint, or Pen for Mouth
Eyes

Inner Ears
Cut 2 Pink

Ears
Cut 2 Gray

Basic Body: Gray
(See page 8 for directions.)

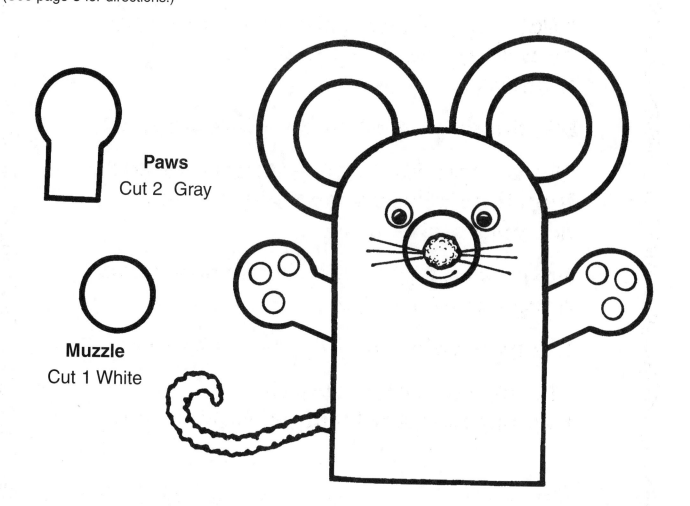

Paws
Cut 2 Gray

Muzzle
Cut 1 White

Attach inner ear circles to centers of ear circles and glue to body by sandwitching between body halves. Sandwich arms between body halves, as shown, and add pink dots to paws. Place pompom nose with whiskers on muzzle. Attach eyes and paint or sew a smile. Attach curled pipe cleaner tail to lower back.

Nine Baby Nightingales

Mother Nightingale's nine baby nightingales napped nicely.

Night was coming. Nightingales wake up at night.

Mother Nightingale's nine baby nightingales napped.

They did not wake up.

"Wake up, baby nightingales. Wake up. Do not nap now!" said Mother Nightingale.

Still the nine baby nightingales napped.

"Help," said Mother Nightingale to Ned Nightingale. "Help me wake my nine napping nightingales."

Now it was night. Ned Nightingale sang a nightingale song.

The nine baby nightingales woke up.

"Thank you. Thank you, Ned Nightingale," said Mother Nightingale.

Using the Letter Nn"

Word Bank

nag	nap	navigate	need	nibble
nip	nix	nod	notice	nourish
nudge	nurse	noodle	nest	nonsense

Activities

1. Bring a "name book" to school. Look up the meaning of each child's name. Make fancy name tags.

2. Discuss things that we "need" to live. Do we need a television set? Do we need food? Do we need water? Do we need toys? Lead the discussion to include many other things we need.

3. Make "nests" from coconut. You need the following supplies: shredded coconut, food coloring, muffin papers, non-stick cooking spray, and an oven. Sprinkle food coloring over the shredded coconut and mix well. Let the coconut dry so the children can handle it without staining their hands. Spray the muffin papers with non-stick cooking spray. Using about ¼ cup coconut, form a nest by pressing the coconut together along the sides of the muffin paper. Bake at 275° F. for 12 to 15 minutes or until dry. Add jelly beans to the nest to resemble eggs.

4. When you see a child doing something "nice" for someone else, point it out to the class. Tell the other children about the nifty act of niceness.

5. Make a "nifty noise maker." For each child to make one you will need two paper plates, paint, paint brushes, beans, and staples. Paint the paper plates. Cover the bottom one with beans. Staple the other plate on the top. Shake for a nifty noise!

Suggested Reading List

Lambert, David. *Birds.* Warwick Press, 1982.

Le Gallienne, Eva. *The Nightingale.* Harper & Row, 1965.

McPhail, David. *David McPhail's Animals A to Z.* Scholastic Inc., 1988.

Reinach, Jacquelyn and Richard Hefter. *Nasty Nightingale.* Holt, Rinehart & Winston, 1977.

Name _____

Phonics Activity

Color the pictures that begin with the **N** sound.

Nn

Ned Nightingale

Nightingale Pattern

Colors: Tan
Brown
Orange

Needs: Eyes

Basic Body: Tan
(See page 8 for directions.)

Wings
Cut 2 Brown

Beak
Cut 1 Orange

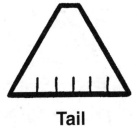

Tail
Cut 1 Brown

Follow the directions for the hen on page 48, omitting the comb and feet.

Olives on Pizza

Ogden Octopus liked olives.

Oliver Octopus did not like olives.

Ogden Octopus and Oliver Octopus made a pizza.

"Stop," said Ogden Octopus. "Do not cook the pizza. I like olives."

"No," said Oliver Octopus. "I do not like olives."

"Olives," said Ogden Octopus.

"No olives," said Oliver Octopus.

"Yes, olives," said Ogden Octopus.

"No, no olives," said Oliver Octopus.

"I know what to do," said Ogden Octopus. "Make some pizza with olives. Make some pizza with no olives."

They were happy. Ogden Octopus ate pizza with olives. Oliver Octopus ate pizza without olives.

Using the Letter "Oo"

Word Bank

object	observe	obtain	occupy	offend
offer	oppose	operate	organize	obey
olive	ostrich	oily	ordinary	outside

Activities

1. Make an "octopus." Use construction paper, paper plates, scissors, and glue. Cut and glue construction paper eyes and arms onto the paper plate. Use all colors of construction paper for arms since an octopus changes colors to blend in with its environment.

2. Count the arms of an "octopus." What could the children do with eight arms? Discuss the possibilities.

3. Discuss a variety of "occupations." If possible, invite guest speakers to share information about their occupations. Culminate the study by having a "Dress Up Day" in which everyone dresses up to represent an occupation, such as firefighter, doctor, astronaut, dancer, or office worker.

4. Practice "on and off." Bring a suitcase of old clothing. Have a relay race to see how quickly the children can put the clothes on and off and put them back in the suitcase.

5. Talk about "opposites." Practice recognizing opposites such as up/down, open/closed, dark/light, sad/happy. Make a sad/happy face from a paper plate. On one side draw a happy face, on the other draw a sad face. Turn the plate over to change the expression from sad to happy.

Suggested Reading List

Brandenberg, Franz. *Otto Is Different.* Greenwillow Books, 1985.

Carrick, Carol. *Octopus.* A Clarion Book—The Seabury Press, 1978.

Heller, Ruth. *How to Hide an Octopus & Other Sea Creatures.* Grosset & Dunlop, 1985.

Lauber, Patricia. *An Octopus Is Amazing.* Thomas Y. Crowell, 1990.

Reese, Bob. *Spongee Sponge.* Children's Press, 1983.

Name _____

Phonics Activity

Color the pictures that begin with the **O** sound.

Oliver Octopus

Octopus Pattern

Colors: Light Pink
            Red

Needs: Eyes
            32 Pink Circles (hole punches or sequins)

Basic Body: Light Pink
(See page 8 for directions.)

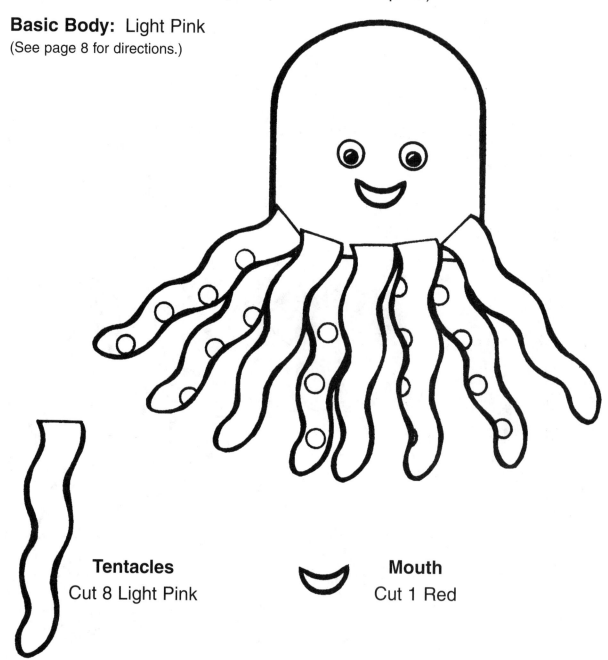

Tentacles
Cut 8 Light Pink

Mouth
Cut 1 Red

Cut about one inch off of the bottom of the basic body and attach arms around bottom edge. Attach four circles to each tentacle for suckers (optional). Glue eyes and legs as shown.

The Pigs Have A Picnic

Pablo and Polly Pig's parents planned a picnic.

"Prepare for the picnic," said Papa and Mama Pig.

Pitter-patter. Pitter-patter. Pablo and Polly Pig prepared for the picnic.

Pablo and Polly Pig packed the picnic lunch.

Papa and Mama Pig said, "Please, pack pears and pizza."

Pablo and Polly Pig packed pears and pizza in the picnic lunch.

Pitter-patter. Pitter-patter. Off went Pablo and Polly Pig for a picnic. Off went Papa and Mama Pig for a picnic.

Pablo and Polly Pig ate lots of pears and pizza. Papa and Mama Pig ate lots of pears and pizza.

What a perfect picnic day!

Using the Letter "Pp"

Word Bank

paddle	paint	parade	party	pass
pay	perform	pester	pick	pediatrician
pebble	peace	pavement	patient	piggyback

Activities

1. Recite the "This Little Piggy" rhyme. Have the children take off their shoes and socks, then say the poem. Make outlines of the children's feet. Compare how they look with other children's outlines. Dip toes (piggies) into finger paint. Make piggie prints (toe prints).

2. Play a "pretend" game. Go on a pretend trip to paradise. Each child needs to think of a P item to take to paradise. List these on the board. Decide which items are practical, pretty, or pleasing.

3. Find pictures of "people" in magazines. Talk about the differences and similarities in people, because of their ages, occupations, dwelling in cities or rural areas, and different countries and/or cultures.

4. Ask a "police officer" to visit the class and explain his or her job.

5. Celebrate the letter P with a "Pink and Purple Party." Everyone should come to school wearing something pink or purple. Make pink and purple party hats and place mats. Serve pink punch, pineapple, peanuts, and pretzels. Play Pin the Tail on the Pig. Make a large pig figure and a tail for each child. To make party hats you will need 9" (23 cm) paper plates, pink and purple tissue paper, paper punch, yarn, and glue. Glue 1" x 4" (2.54 cm x 10 cm) strips of pink and/or purple tissue paper around the edge of the plate for fringe. Glue pink and/or purple tissue paper squares to the bottom side of the plate. Punch holes on opposite sides of the plate. Attach yarn so the hat can be tied under the chin. The bottom of the plate becomes the top of the hat.

Suggested Reading List

Getz, Arthur. *Humphrey, The Dancing Pig.* The Dial Press, 1980.

Hellard, Susan. *This Little Piggy.* G.P. Putnam's Sons, 1989.

Marshall, James. *The Three Little Pigs.* Penguin, 1989.

Stolz, Mary. *Emmett Pig.* Harper & Row, 1959.

Van Leeuwen, Jean. *Tales of Amanda Pig.* Dial, 1983.

Name _____

Phonics Activity

Color the pictures that begin with the **P** sound.

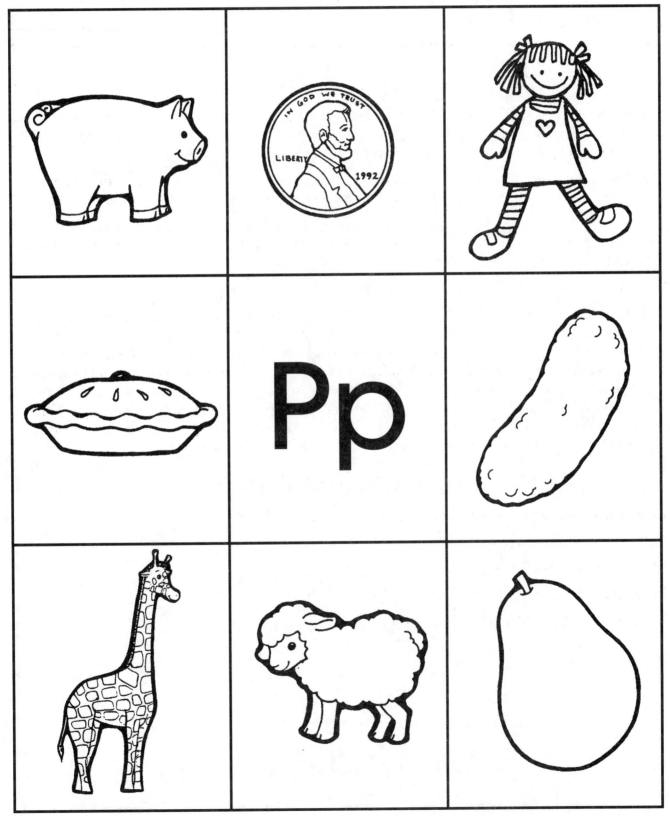

Pp

Pablo and Polly Pig

Pig Pattern

Colors: Pink
Red
Dark Brown

Needs: 1 Pink Pompom
1 Pink Pipe Cleaner (1½")
Eyes

Basic Body: Pink
(See page 8 for directions.)

Mouth
Cut 1 Red

Hooves
Cut 2 Pink

Ears
Cut 2 Pink

Nostrils
Cut 2 Dark Brown

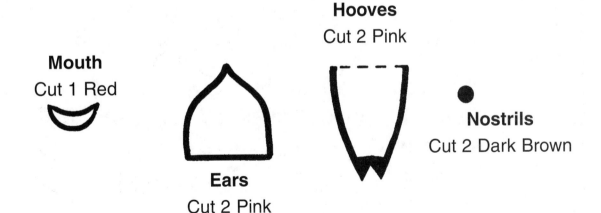

Sandwich ears and hooves between body halves as shown. Glue 2 nostrils to pompom for nose and glue to center of face. Add eyes and mouth. Attach a curled pipe cleaner to lower back for tail.

What Quacks?

Quentin Quail quickly ran home.

Mother Quail said, "Quentin Quail, why do you run so quickly?"

Quentin Quail hid under a quilt.

"Why do you hide under a quilt, Quentin Quail?" asked Mother Quail.

"I am afraid," said Quentin Quail.

"Something said quack, quack."

"Quentin Quail, you do not have to be afraid," Mother Quail said. "Ducks say quack, quack."

Quentin Quail came out from under the quilt. "Ducks quack?" he asked.

"Yes, ducks quack," said Mother Quail. Quentin Quail was not afraid.

He quickly ran outside. He could hear "quack, quack, quack." Quentin was not afraid!

Using the Letter "Qq"

Word Bank

quake	quality	quell	quench	question
quicken	quit	quiet	quack	quibble
quote	quite	quilt	quarter	quartz

Activities

1. Measure "quarts" of water. Color the water with several drops of food coloring. Have the children estimate how many cups of water would fit into a quart jar. Pour in the cups of water until the jar is full. Also measure quarts of fruit, sand, salt, or candy.

2. Bring some "quarters" to class. Help the children identify the quarters as money. Explain that the quarter is worth more than a penny, nickel, or dime. Put out other coins and help the children identify the quarter.

3. Bring in pieces of "quartz" for the children to examine. Look at the quartz using a magnifying glass. Talk about how it is used.

4. Use a feather to write. Make your own "quill pen" by dipping the base end of the feather into some paint. Write on a piece of painting paper. Be sure to have the children wear paint shirts.

5. Make a "Q quilt." An old sheet cut into squares works well. Let each child decorate a square with a picture of something that begins with Q. If there are many children in the class, let them work in groups. Use felt pens or fabric paint to illustrate their Q design. Ask for a parent volunteer to sew the quilt squares together. If it is not possible for you to use fabric, make the quilt from pieces of construction paper. Fasten the squares together with yarn threaded through punched holes or with tape. Display the quilt on the Q bulletin board.

Suggested Reading List

Haley, Neal. *Birds for Pets and Pleasure.* Delacort Press, 1981.

McPhail, David. *David McPhail's Animals A to Z.* Scholastic, 1988.

Stranger, Margaret A. *That Quail, Robert.* J.B. Lippincot, 1966.

Upvardy, Miklos D.F. *The Audubon Society Field Guide to North American Birds.* Alfred A. Knopf, 1977.

Name _____

Phonics Activity

Color the pictures that begin with the **Q** sound.

Qq

Quentin Quail

Quail Pattern

Colors: Brown
Tan
Blue
White
Yellow

Needs: Eyes

Basic Body: Tan
(See page 8 for directions.)

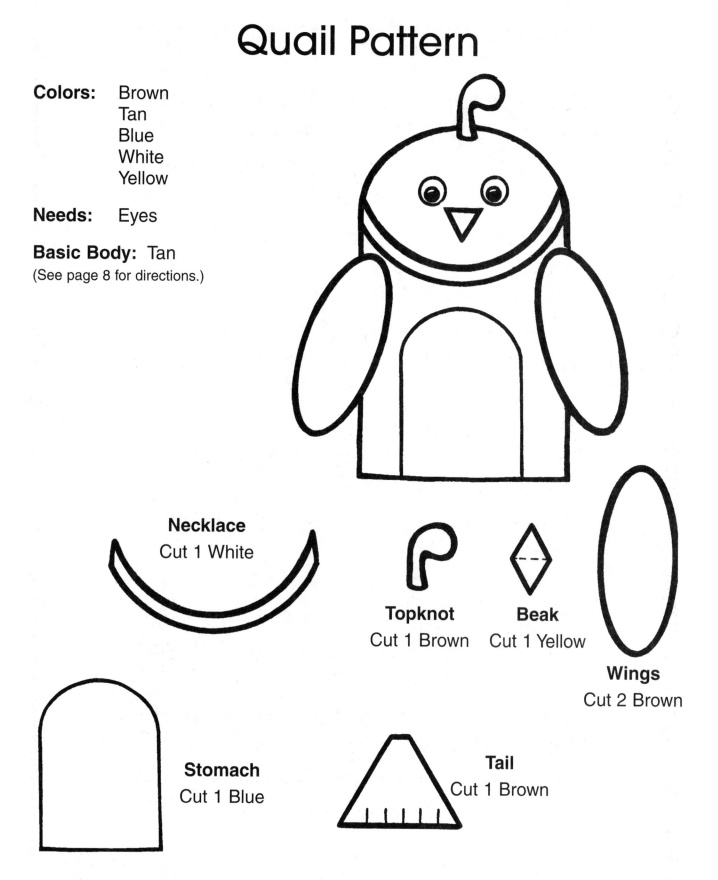

Necklace
Cut 1 White

Topknot
Cut 1 Brown

Beak
Cut 1 Yellow

Wings
Cut 2 Brown

Stomach
Cut 1 Blue

Tail
Cut 1 Brown

Following the illustration glue the necklace and stomach to basic body. Glue remaining features into place with the tail at the lower back. Glue beak as for hen on page 48.

"I Want A Raw Carrot!"

Ricky Rabbit was really hungry. He wanted a raw carrot to eat.

Ricky Rabbit ran to the refrigerator. He saw a raw red radish.

"I want a raw carrot," said Ricky Rabbit.
"I really want a raw carrot!"

Ricky Rabbit sat right down by the refrigerator and cried. He cried really loudly!

Mother Rabbit ran to Ricky Rabbit. "Why are you crying really loudly?" asked Mother Rabbit.

"I am really hungry," said Ricky Rabbit.
"I want a raw carrot to eat."

"Ricky Rabbit, " said Mother Rabbit, "do not cry really loudly. We can get you a raw carrot from the garden."

Ricky Rabbit ran to the garden. Mother Rabbit got him a raw carrot.

"Thank you, Mother Rabbit," said Ricky Rabbit. He was really happy.

Using the Letter "Rr"

Word Bank

race	ramble	read	reason	redo
remove	repair	resist	rip	rush
round	responsible	ribbon	rocket	radio

Activities

1. Study "railroad" crossing signs. Discuss how to be safe while near railroad tracks. Make a human train and travel around the room. With arms bent at the elbows, move arms up and down in a circular motion. Be sure to make chugging and whistling sounds as you go.

2. Celebrate "reading!" Have students bring a sleeping bag or blanket, pillow, and their favorite books to school for a day. Spread out on the floor and read.

3. Have a "Ridiculous Red Day." Each child should wear something red to school. Clothes can be crazy and creative. Drink red punch. Eat red apples and red licorice. Write with red crayon.

4. Clap out a "rhythm" pattern, for example: two quick claps, pause, two quick claps. Have the children repeat the rhythm pattern. Let the children have turns making up a pattern for the others to repeat. Use rulers or rocks to tap out a rhythm.

5. Take an opportunity to discuss "rules." There are many rules in our lives that are important for children to know. Talk about classroom rules, school rules, fire safety rules, traffic rules, and bicycle rules.

Suggested Reading List

DeBall-Kwitz, Mary. *Rabbits' Search for a Little House.* Crown, 1977.

Dunn, Judy. *The Little Rabbit.* Random House, 1980.

Gackenback, Dick. *Hattie Rabbit.* Harper & Row, 1976.

Ketchum Murrow, Lisa. *Good-bye, Sammy.* Holiday House, 1989.

Wahl, Jan. *Carrot Nose.* Eastern Press, 1978.

Phonics Activity

Color the pictures that begin with the **R** sound.

Rr

Ricky Rabbit

Rabbit Pattern

Colors: White
Pink

Needs: Eyes
Thread for Whiskers
6 Pink "hole punched" dots
1 White Pompom

Basic Body: White
(See page 8 for directions.)

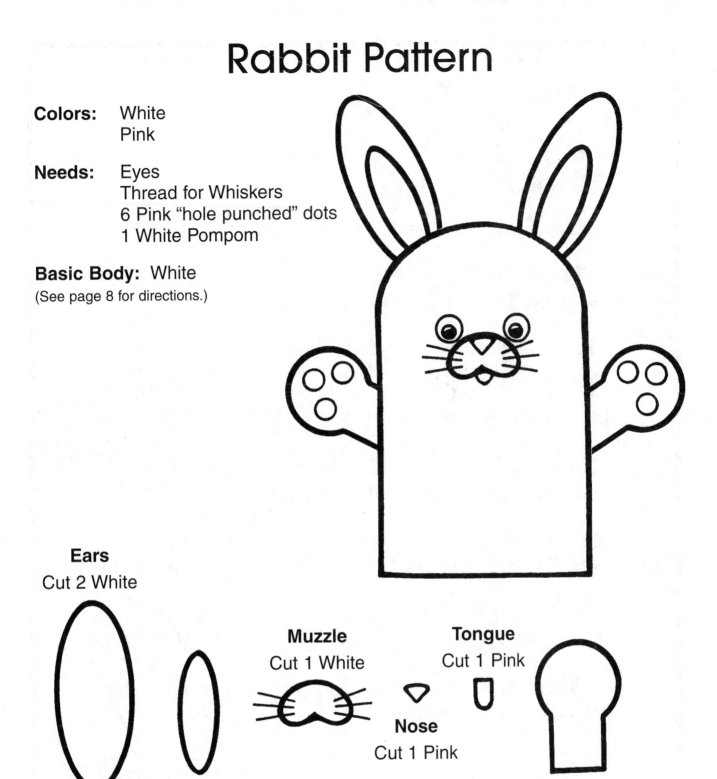

Ears
Cut 2 White

Inner Ears
Cut 2 Pink

Muzzle
Cut 1 White

Nose
Cut 1 Pink

Tongue
Cut 1 Pink

Paws
Cut 2 White

Glue inner ears to ears and sandwich between body halves. Sandwich paws as well. Attach tongue behind muzzle. Glue nose and whiskers to muzzle, and glue muzzle to body. Add three punched dots to each paw as shown. Glue pompom to lower back of body. Add eyes.

Sally Sue, Sandy Sue, and The Skunk

Sally Sue and Sandy Sue were sisters walking to school.

Sally Sue stopped. "Smell, Sandy Sue!"

"Skunk," said Sandy Sue. "A smelly skunk! This skunk is too close!"

Sally Sue and Sandy Sue hid by a sand hill. A snail hid by the sand hill, too.

The smelly skunk strolled by the sand hill.

The snail smashed his nose. "Skunks are super, super smelly!" said the snail.

Sally Sue and Sandy Sue smiled. "Yes," said Sally Sue. "Skunks are super smelly."

"The skunk is gone," said Sandy Sue. "We have to go to school."

"Good-bye, Snail," said the sisters as they strolled to school.

Using the Letter "Ss"

Word Bank

say	scamper	scoop	search	sing
sleep	sneak	spill	step	sweet
strong	silent	scarf	stomach	submarine

Activities

1. Let each child decorate a "sack" in which to keep his/her S papers and other S items. Color on lunch size bags or cut shapes from construction paper and glue them to the bag.

2. Discuss traffic "safety." Talk about safely crossing the street, and seat belt safety. Make traffic lights using 12" x 24" (30cm x 61cm) black construction paper, 9" x 12" (23cm x 30cm) red, yellow and green construction paper, scissors, and glue. Use the black paper for the background. Cut large red, yellow and green circles for the lights. Glue the circles on the black paper from the top, red, yellow, and green.

3. Play the "secret telephone" game. Place the children in a long line. Whisper a secret using lots of S words into the ear of the first child. That child then whispers the secret to the second child and so on. The last child repeats the secret out loud. The secret may be different by the time it reaches the end of the line!

4. Make "snowflakes" to hang from the ceiling and on the windows. Typing paper is easier to cut than construction paper when folding and cutting. Fold into six sections before cutting.

5. Use a circle of yellow construction paper for the center of a "sun." Cut 1" x 6" (2.54 cm x 15 cm) strips of yellow construction paper. Curl the strips on a pencil and glue to the perimeter of the circle to make the rays of the sun.

Suggested Reading List

De Ford, Deborah. *I Wonder Why Skunks Are So Smelly And Other Neat Facts About Mammals.* Golden Books, 1992.

Hess, Lolo. *The Misunderstood Skunk.* Charles Scriboer's Sons, 1969.

Pelavin, Cheryl. *Ruby's Revenge.* G.P. Putnam's Sons, 1972.

Reese, Ron. *Sammy Skunk.* Aro Publishing Company, 1984.

Stevens, Carla. *Rabbit and Skunk and the Scary Rock.* Scholastic, 1962.

Name _____

Phonics Activity

Color the pictures that begin with the **S** sound.

Ss

Super Smelly Skunk

103

Skunk Pattern

Colors: Black
White

Needs: Eyes
1 Pink Pompom
Thread for Whiskers

Basic Body: Black
(See page 8 for directions.)

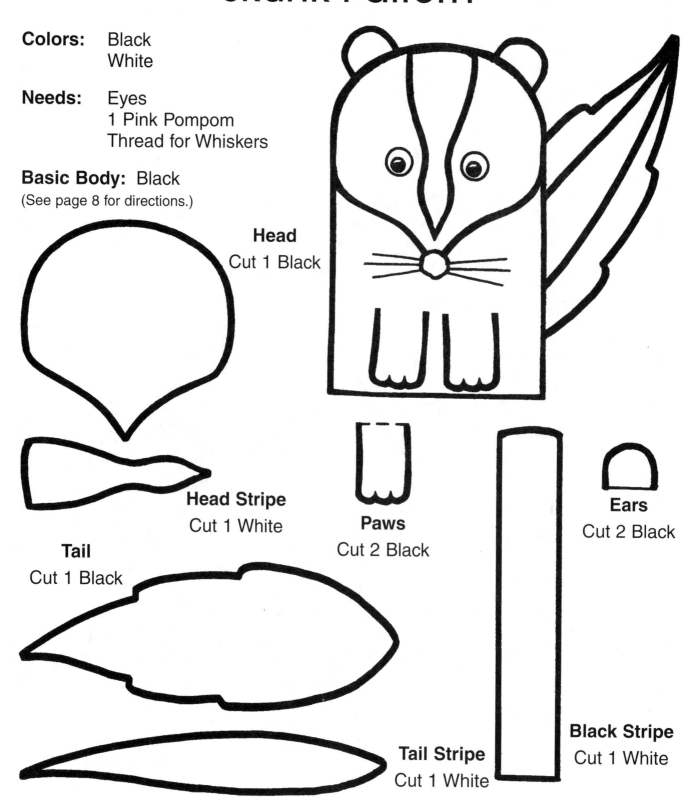

Head
Cut 1 Black

Head Stripe
Cut 1 White

Paws
Cut 2 Black

Ears
Cut 2 Black

Tail
Cut 1 Black

Tail Stripe
Cut 1 White

Black Stripe
Cut 1 White

Attach ears between body halves. Glue head to body. Decorate head, backside, and tail with appropriate stripes and glue in place. Glue whiskers to tip of muzzle and place pompom nose on top. Glue remaining features as shown.

Ted Turtle and the Tall Boy

Ted Turtle liked to swim in the pond. He could swim fast.

One day a tall boy took Ted Turtle away from the pond.

The tall boy took Ted Turtle to a tent. The boy ate toast and tea.

The tall boy tried to give Ted Turtle toast and tea. Ted Turtle hid.

The tall boy went to sleep in the tent. Ted Turtle did not sleep.

Ted Turtle wanted to go home. Ted Turtle wanted to swim in the pond.

Ted Turtle tried to hurry. He was slow. Ted Turtle walked all night.

He came to the pond. Ted Turtle swam away fast!

The water tickled Ted Turtle's tummy. He laughed and was glad to be home!

Using the Letter "Tt"

Word Bank

tackle	tag	talk	teach	tickle
tip	trip	toss	trade	trick
temporary	tall	total	town	tunnel

Activities

1. Bring a variety of foods to school for the children to "taste." Try to bring unusual foods as well as common foods. The produce section of your grocery store will give you some uncommon ideas. Discuss with the children the way each item tastes. Did they like it? Describe the taste using tasty, tart, terrible, tingly, and tame rather than good and bad.

2. Use an old or "toy telephone" to teach the children good telephone answering manners. Teach them to lay the telephone down to get someone else to answer it rather than shouting to the person. Always ask politely who is calling. The children should never tell the caller that they are alone.

3. Set up a small pup "tent" in the classroom. Place a variety of items and books that begin with T inside the tent. Allow the children to explore the tent.

4. Put a variety of items (or one at a time for younger children) in a bag without the children seeing the items. Call the children up one at a time to "touch the things" in the bag. They must try to figure out what each item is just by touching it. When all the children have touched the items and you have discussed the possibilities of what they might be, show the items to the children. How accurate was their sense of touch?

5. Make a "tree" bulletin board. Cut a large "trunk" from brown butcher paper. Have the children cut leaves from green construction paper. Write one word that begins with T on each leaf before putting it on the tree.

Suggested Reading List

Ancona, George. *Turtle Watch.* Macmillan, 1987.

Kessler, Leonard. *Old Turtle's Soccer Team.* Greenwillow, 1988.

Maris, Ron. *I Wish I Could Fly.* Greenwillow, 1986.

Skryja, David. *The Turtle.* Raintree Publishers, 1986.

Waters, John F. *Green Turtle Mysteries.* Thomas Y. Crowell, 1972.

Name _____

Phonics Activity

Color the pictures that begin with the **T** sound.

Tt

Ted Turtle

Turtle Pattern

Colors: Dark Green
Light Green

Needs: Eyes

Basic Body: Dark Green
(See page 8 for directions.)

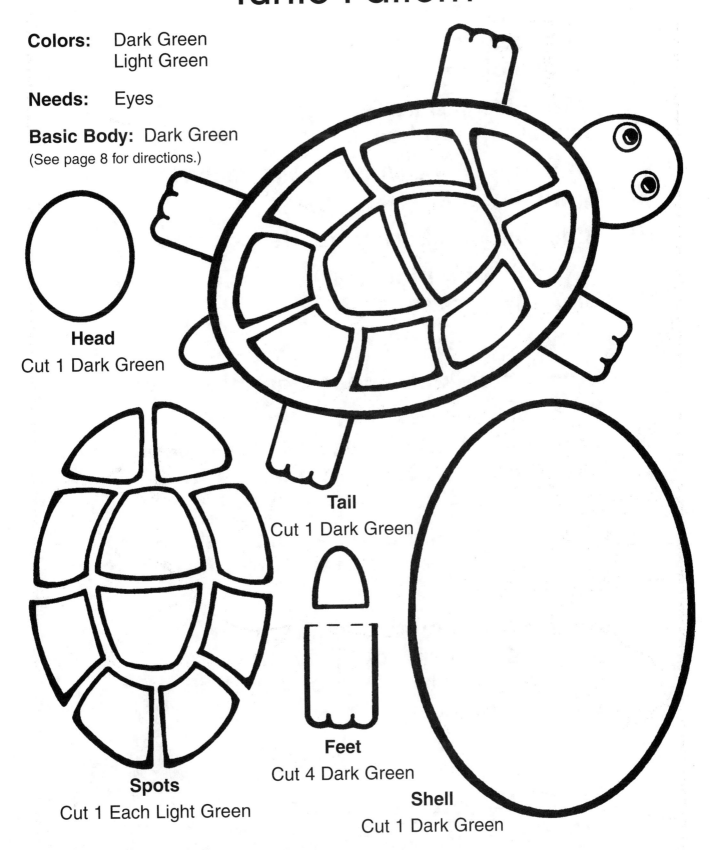

Head
Cut 1 Dark Green

Tail
Cut 1 Dark Green

Feet
Cut 4 Dark Green

Spots
Cut 1 Each Light Green

Shell
Cut 1 Dark Green

Glue the shell spots onto the shell as shown in illustration. Glue the legs as shown in illustration. Glue the head and tail into place. Glue the shell to the basic body positioning the tail over the body opening.

The Umbrellabird's Feather

"This is unusual," said Ulric Umbrellabird.

"My umbrellabird feather is not black. Usually my feathers are all black."

"This one is not black," said Ursula Umbrellabird.

Ulric Umbrellabird cried. He was upset.

"I will color it black," said Ursula Umbrellabird.

"What will I use?"

Ulric Umbrellabird cried and cried. He was very upset.

Ursula Umbrellabird used black crayon. The feather did not turn black. Ulric Umbrellabird cried some more.

Ursula Umbrellabird used black shoe polish. Now Ulric Umbrellabird's feather was black!

Ulric Umbrellabird was happy. He laughed. "Thank you, Ursula Umbrellabird. Now my feather is its usual color!"

Using the Letter "Uu"

Word Bank

unfold	unmask	understand	undo	undertake
unwrap	untwist	uplift	usher	utter
umbrella	unsaddle	upstairs	under	up

Activities

1. Open an "umbrella" and suspend it from the ceiling of your room. Whenever you hear a word that has a U in it, write the word on an index card. Put the card in the umbrella. At the end of the day, remove the word cards, count them and give an unusual hooray for each one.

2. Practice "under." Caution the children to follow directions carefully. Give each of them a piece of paper and ask them to draw a square at the top of the page. Then ask them to draw a triangle under the square. The activity can be continued as you ask the children to draw one shape under the other. Another way to practice "under" is to do the limbo dance. Use a string or measuring stick, and lower it after each child has gone under. Play music during the dance.

3. Study some animals that live "underground." Ants, worms, or gophers would be interesting.

4. Discuss things that make people "unhappy." Allow the children to illustrate pictures showing a time or situation in which they were unhappy. Practice showing each other happy and unhappy faces.

5. Bring various items of clothing, linens, and shoes to school. Have the children practice folding and "unfolding," zipping and "unzipping," buttoning and "unbuttoning," lacing and "unlacing," tying and "untying."

Suggested Reading List

Argent, Kerry. *Animal Capers.* Dial Books, 1989.

Lenga, Rosalind. *The Amazing Fact Book of Birds.* A & P Books/Creative Education, 1979.

Kitchen, Bert. *Animal Alphabet.* Dial Books, 1984.

Platt, Kin. *Big Max.* Harper & Row, 1965.

Yashima, Taro. *Umbrella.* Puffin Books, 1958.

Phonics Activity

Color the pictures that begin with the **U** sound.

Uu

Black Shoe Polish

Ulric Umbrellabird

Umbrellabird Pattern

Colors: Black
             Orange

Needs: Four 1/4" (.6 cm) Black Pompoms
             Eyes

Basic Body: Black
(See page 8 for directions.)

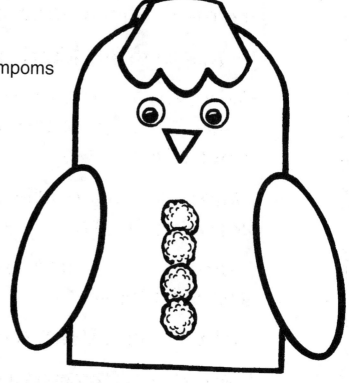

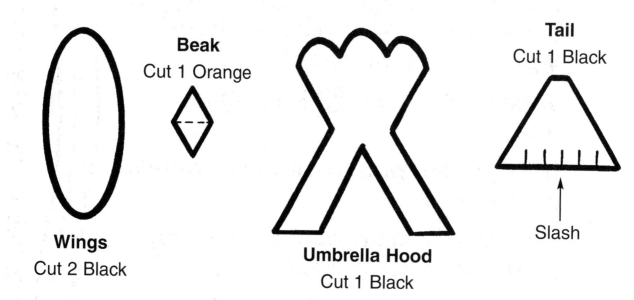

Wings
Cut 2 Black

Beak
Cut 1 Orange

Umbrella Hood
Cut 1 Black

Tail
Cut 1 Black

Slash

The umbrella hood's large V is glued to the rounded portion of the basic body. The inside edges of the V are brought together before gluing forming the hood that comes over the front of the head. Glue the remaining features.

Purple And Blue Violets

Veronica Viper liked purple violets.

Vanessa Viper liked blue violets.

Veronica Viper put purple violets in a vase. Vanessa Viper put blue violets in a vase.

"Mine are the prettiest violets," said Veronica Viper.

"Mine are the prettiest violets," said Vanessa Viper.

"Mine!" said Veronica Viper.

"Mine!" said Vanessa Viper.

One long viper tail bumped the vases. One vase broke. Veronica Viper said, "I am sorry."

Vanessa Viper said, "I am sorry, too."

They put the purple and blue violets in one vase.

"Purple and blue violets are pretty in one vase," they said.

Veronica Viper and Vanessa Viper were happy.

Using the Letter "Vv"

Word Bank

value	vandalize	vision	vent	verify
veto	violate	visit	vocalize	volunteer
vote	voluntary	vital	vein	violin

Activities

1. Pretend to take a "vacation" with your class. Bring beach blankets, a picnic lunch, and pictures of the beach for a warm weather vacation. Pretend to swim and roast marshmallows. A pretend vacation can be taken anywhere. Just bring in a few props and a lot of imagination.

2. Bring a "variety of vegetables" to school. Discuss them. Eat the vegetables and then make a collage of vegetables. Do this by cutting out pictures of vegetables and gluing them to a large piece of butcher paper that is cut into the shape of a vegetable.

3. Ask several of the children's parents to "visit" your class to read a story. The visitors should dress up as one of the characters in the book that they will read. Prepare the children for the visit by telling them that a special visitor will be coming to the class. Excitement and expectation will build if you provide some mystery as you prepare the children for visitors.

4. Talk about "vision. " Explain that vision is the sense of sight. Show the children pictures and models of the eyes. Have the children illustrate the eye. Discuss ways that blind people "see."

5. Make "vipers" by stuffing nylon stockings with polyester filling. Tie the open end with string or a rubber band. Add eyes and back markings with a marking pen.

Suggested Reading List

Barger, Sherie and Linda Johnson. *Tree Vipers.* Rourke Enterprises, 1987.

Barrett, Norman. *Picture Library Snakes.* Franklin Watts, 1989.

Fichter, George S. *Snakes Around the World.* Franklin Watts, 1980.

Freedman, Russell. *Killer Snakes.* Holiday House, 1982.

Wexo, John Bonnett. *Snakes.* Creative Education, Inc., 1987.

Phonics Activity

Color the pictures that begin with the **V** sound.

Vv

Veronica and Vanessa Viper

Viper Pattern

Colors: Red
Dark Green
Light Green
White

Needs: Eyes

Basic Body: Dark Green
(See page 8 for directions.)

Tongue
Cut 1 Red

Fangs
Cut 2 White

Tail
Cut 1 Dark Green

Head
Cut 1 Light Green

Diamond
Cut 1 Light Green

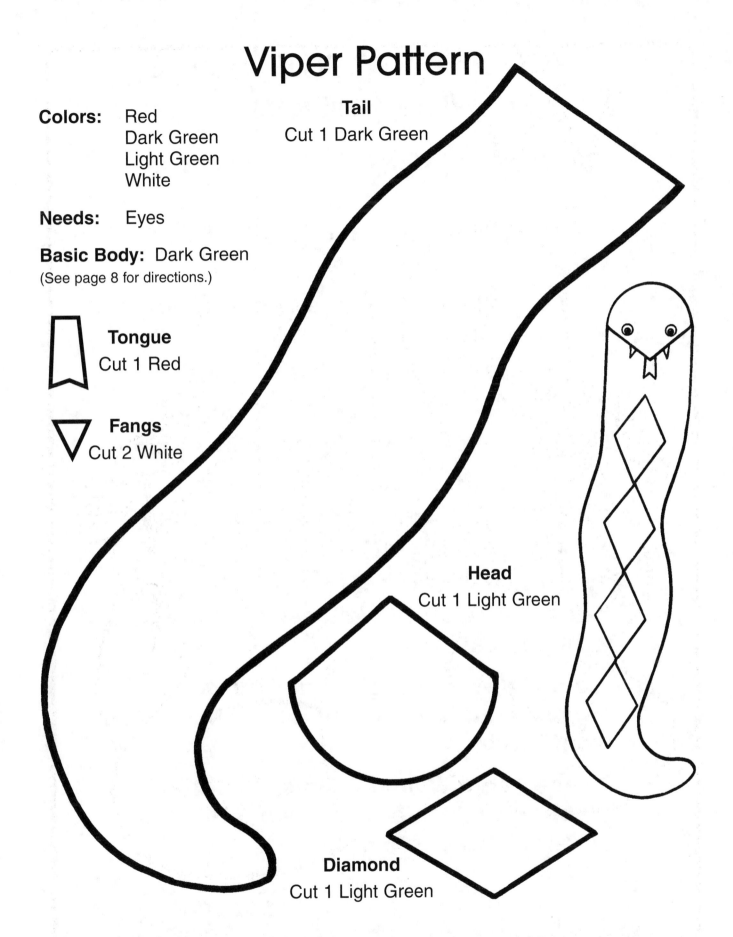

Glue the diamonds to the tail. Attach to basic body. Position the fangs and tongue behind the head. Glue on eyes. Attach the head to the basic body.

Woodrow Walrus Wants Watermelon

Woodrow and Winnie Walrus waded in the water.

"That's weird," said Woodrow Walrus. "I want watermelon."

"Watermelon is not in the water," said Winnie Walrus.

Woodrow Walrus said, "That's weird. I want watermelon to eat."

"Walruses do not eat watermelon," said Winnie Walrus.

"That's weird. I want watermelon," said Woodrow Walrus again.

"Woodrow Walrus," said Winnie Walrus. "Walruses eat fish! Walruses do not eat watermelon!"

Woodrow Walrus looked at Winnie Walrus. "That's weird," he said. "Now I want fish."

"Good," said Winnie Walrus. Woodrow Walrus and Winnie Walrus waded in the water to find fish to eat.

Using the Letter "Ww"

Word Bank

wade	wag	wait	wander	wash
wave	wear	weigh	wobble	warm
water	wonderful	weather	wish	winter

Activities

1. Fill a "wagon" with "w" items. Have the children watch as you look at the items and discuss "w." Let the children pull the wagon while walking, watching, and winking.

2. Play Simon Says. As Simon, ask the children to "walk" slowly, forward, and backward. Ask them to wiggle, wave, wag, wink, wipe, and face west.

3. Learn the days of the "week." Each day ask the children to tell you what day is today, what day yesterday was and what day tomorrow is going to be. Make week books by illustrating an important happening for each day of the week.

4. Make a "window." For each child you will need one 9" x 12" (23cm x 30cm) piece of construction paper, one 8" x 11" (20cm x 28cm) piece of cellophane, decorations, scissors and glue. Have children cut the center out of the construction paper to form a frame. Glue the cellophane to the back of the construction paper frame that is wide enough to decorate. Decorate the frame as desired.

5. Discuss the season of "winter." Bring items that we use in the winter such as hats, mittens, sleds, shovels, and ice scrapers. Discuss why winter is different in the different parts of the country. Talk about why it would be inappropriate to wear summer clothing in the winter weather and winter clothing in summer weather.

Suggested Reading List

Darling, Kathy. *Walrus on Location.* Lothrop, Lee & Shepard, 1991.

Green, Carl R. and William R. Sanford. *The Walrus.* Crestwood House, 1986.

Hefter, Richard. *Very Worried Walrus.* Holt, Rinehart and Winston, 1977.

McDearmon, Kay. *The Walrus Giant of the Arctic Ice.* Dodd, Mead & Company, 1974.

Wexo, John Bonnett. *Seals, Sea Lions & Walruses.* Creative Education, Inc., 1987.

Name _____

Phonics Activity

Color the pictures that begin with the **W** sound.

Ww

Woodrow Walrus

Walrus Pattern

Colors: Tan
Brown
Black
White

Needs: Thread for Whiskers
Eyes

Basic Body: Tan
(See page 8 for directions.)

Ears
Cut 2 Tan

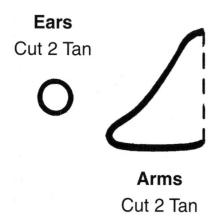

Arms
Cut 2 Tan

Muzzle
Cut 1 Brown

Tusks
Cut 2 White

Nostrils
Cut 2 Black

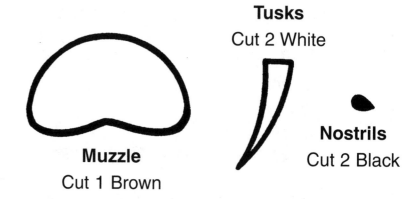

Position the muzzle and tusks on the face so that the pointed ends of the tusks are just above the open edge of the basic body. Glue into place. Place three ½" threads on each side of the muzzle. Glue the nostrils above the threads. Put ears and arms between the halves of the basic body.

A Box For Dixie Fox

"Alex," said Dixie Fox, "please, fix my box."

"How can I fix your box?" asked Alex Fox. "I do not know how to fix a box."

Dixie Fox was sad. Alex Fox did now know how to fix her box.

"Mr. Ox may have another box at his store," said Alex Fox.

Alex Fox and Dixie Fox went to see Mr. Ox.

"Mr. Ox," said Alex Fox. "I do not know how to fix Dixie's box. Do you have another box?"

Mr. Ox had six boxes at his store!

"Oh," said Dixie Fox, "Alex, help me choose a box."

"Box number six has a fox on it. Choose it, Dixie," said Alex Fox.

"Yes, I want box number six," said Dixie Fox. She was very happy.

Using the Letter "Xx"

Word Bank

exit	exhaust	expect	experiment	explode
explore	express	extend	fix	mix
nix	tax	fox	taxi	oxygen

Activities

Note: Be aware that "x" has two distinctive sounds. "X" sounds like "z" at the beginning of words such as xylophone. The more common "ks" sound is found within or at the end of words or syllables, such as expect, fox and tuxedo. The "ks" sound is more common, and so it is highlighted here.

1. Look at road signs that have an "X" on them. Railroad crossing and school crossing signs often have an "X" on them. Talk about the importance of such signs and why they should be obeyed.

2. Bring an "x-ray" to the classroom. Discuss how an x-ray is taken and how and why it is used. Let children talk about having x-rays taken.

3. For an "extra special" art center project glue two craft sticks together into an X and decorate.

4. Using a large plain "box," have the children decorate it using yarn, crayons, markers, packing peanuts, etc. This will be the class X box. All decorating should be done in the shape of an X. Have the children collect items in the box that have the X (ks) sound.

5. Play tic-tac-toe using "X's" and "O's." Using a large grid on the chalkboard, show children how to play. As an extension, make large grids out of masking tape on the floor. Provide children with O's cut out of paper or large rubber bands. Let them use the X's made in #3 above to play the game.

Suggested Reading List

Barbaresi, Nina. *A Fox Jumped Up One Winter's Night.* Western, 1985.

Koralek, Jenny. *The Friendly Fox.* Little, Brown and Company, 1988.

Marshall, Edward. *Fox in Love.* Dial, 1982.

Marshall, Edward. *Fox and His Friends.* Dial, 1982.

Tompert, Ann. *Little Fox Goes to the End of the World.* Crown, 1976.

Name _____

Phonics Activity

Color the pictures that have the **X** sound.

Xx

Dixie Fox

128

Fox Pattern

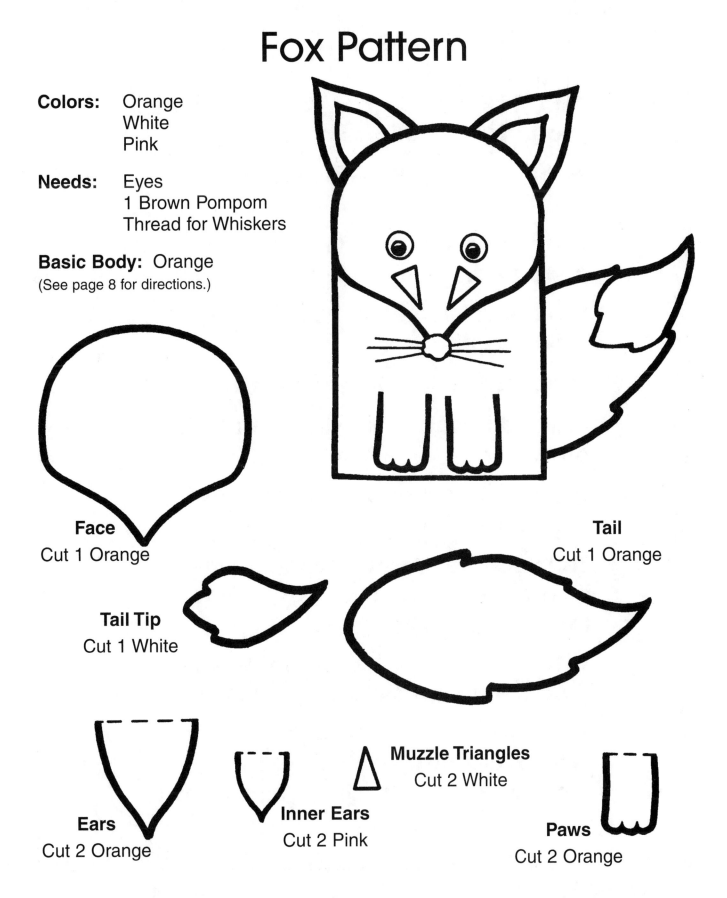

Colors: Orange
White
Pink

Needs: Eyes
1 Brown Pompom
Thread for Whiskers

Basic Body: Orange
(See page 8 for directions.)

Face
Cut 1 Orange

Tail Tip
Cut 1 White

Tail
Cut 1 Orange

Ears
Cut 2 Orange

Inner Ears
Cut 2 Pink

Muzzle Triangles
Cut 2 White

Paws
Cut 2 Orange

Position three 1½" thread where the nose will be. Glue the pompom over the threads for nose. Glue remaining features into place following illustration. Glue white tip to the end of the tail and glue to lower back of the body.

Yetta Yak's Yellow Bowl

Yetta Yak was hungry. Yetta Yak liked yogurt in her yellow bowl.

"Where is my yellow bowl?" asked Yetta Yak.

Yetta Yak looked in her yellow cupboard.

There was no yellow bowl in the yellow cupboard.

Yetta Yak looked in her yellow sink.

"Yuk," she said. "My yellow bowl is dirty."

Yetta Yak washed her yellow bowl in her yellow sink.

Yetta Yak put yogurt in her yellow bowl. "Yum, yum, this is good yogurt in my yellow bowl."

Yetta Yak ate all the yogurt. She put her dirty yellow bowl in her yellow sink.

What will Yetta Yak say next time when she finds her dirty yellow bowl?

Using the Letter "Yy"

Word Bank

yammer	yak	yank	yap	yawn
yell	yearn	yelp	yip	yodel
yolk	yowl	young	yesterday	yogurt

Activities

1. Make a "yarn" picture using yellow yarn. Outline the letter Y on a piece of construction paper. Fill in the Y with yellow yarn.

2. Learn the months that make up a "year." Discuss the seasons that are in a year. Illustrate a symbol for each month of the year or draw pictures representing the seasons.

3. Talk about "yesterday." What did you eat for breakfast yesterday? What did you do at school yesterday? Make a mural of the important events that happened yesterday.

4. Bring raw and hard-boiled eggs to school for the children to study. Break some raw eggs onto a plate and look at the "yolks." Crack some hard-boiled eggs and compare the two kinds of "yolks."

5. Tell the children how important each one of them is. Say, "You are a very special, one-of-a-kind person!" Draw the outline of each child on a large piece of butcher paper. Cut out the shapes. Let the children color the shapes so they look like themselves. Name these "You" pictures. Hang these on a special "You" bulletin board. Have the child choose a quality that is special or unique to him or her. Instead of using the name to identify the body shape, use his or her special quality.

Suggested Reading List

Adam, Edith. *The Noisy Book Starring Yakety Yak.* Random, 1983.

Argent, Kerry. *Animal Capers.* Dial, 1989.

Johnson, Odette and Bruce. *Apples, Alligators and also Alphabets.* Oxford University Press, 1990.

Moss, Jeff. *Bob and Jack: A Boy and His Yak.* Bantam Books, 1992.

Seuss, Dr. *Dr. Seuss' ABC.* Random House, 1963.

Name _____

Phonics Activity

Color the pictures that begin with the **Y** sound.

Yy

Yetta Yak

Yak Pattern

Colors: Yellow
Brown
Tan
Dark Brown

Needs: Eyes

Basic Body: Yellow
(See page 8 for directions.)

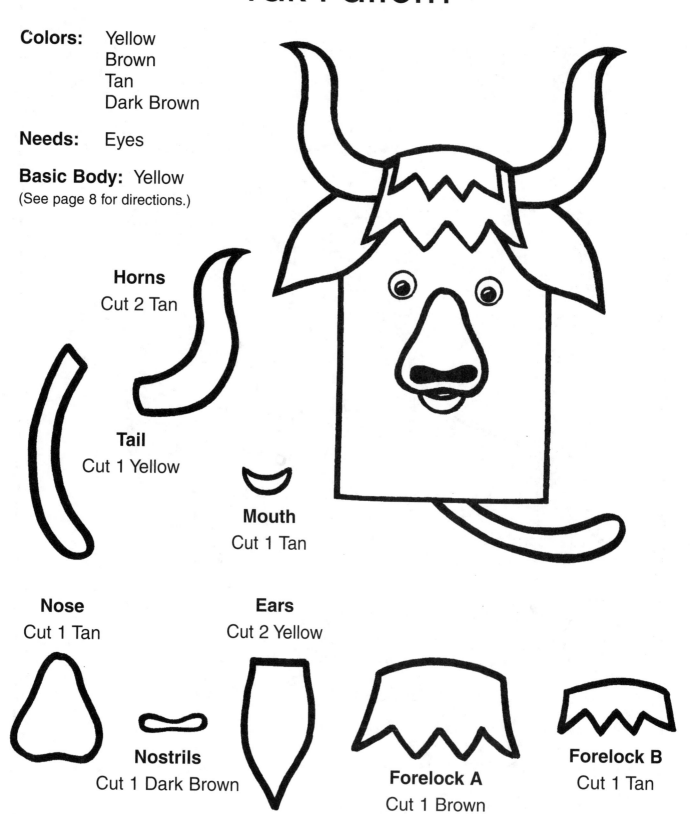

Horns
Cut 2 Tan

Tail
Cut 1 Yellow

Mouth
Cut 1 Tan

Nose
Cut 1 Tan

Nostrils
Cut 1 Dark Brown

Ears
Cut 2 Yellow

Forelock A
Cut 1 Brown

Forelock B
Cut 1 Tan

Glue features into place following illustration. Glue tail to lower back pointing downward.

Zoomy Zed Zebra

Zed Zebra zoomed past Zeke the zookeeper into the barn.

"Zikes!" said Mother Zebra. "Zed Zebra, why do you zip and zoom around so fast?"

Zip, zing! Zed Zebra zoomed out of the zoo barn past Zeke the zookeeper.

"You zoom too fast, little Zed Zebra," said Zeke the zookeeper.

Zip, zing! Little Zed Zebra zoomed into the zoo barn again.

"Zed Zebra, stop!" said Mother Zebra. "Zed Zebra, you zoom too fast."

Zed Zebra stopped. He was tired.

"Little Zed Zebra, you need a zippy nap," said Mother Zebra.

Z-Z-Z-Z-Z-Z. Zip! Little Zed Zebra was fast asleep!

Using the Letter "Zz"

Word Bank

zap	zest	zigzag	zinc	zip
zone	zonk	zoom	zoo	zero
zeal	zany	zipper	zither	zing

Activities

1. Look at a picture of a "zebra." Count the stripes on the zebra. What else do you know about that has stripes?

2. Paint some "zigzag Z's." Stretch a long piece of butcher paper across the room and let the children go to work. If you are concerned about paint spills, use marking pens.

3. Plant "zucchini" seeds and watch them zip out of the soil (grow)!

4. Have a "Zany Dress Day. " Let the children wear something zany to school. You might suggest they wear their clothing backwards or unmatched shoes and socks. Children could also paint their faces (with parental help) and wear zany hairstyles.

5. Create a "Z zone" in the classroom. Fill the area with pictures of things beginning with Z. Provide scissors, crayons, and paper that the children can use to make their own Zs. Mount a long strip of adding machine tape on the wall or floor of the Z zone. The children can write a long line of Zs on the tape.

Suggested Reading List

Argent, Kerry. *Animal Capers.* Dial Books, 1989.

Green, Carl R. and William R. Sanford. *The Zebra.* Crestwood House, 1988.

Irvine, Georgeanne. *Zoo Babies: Zelda the Zebra.* Children's Press, 1982.

Johnston, Odette and Bruce. *Apples, Alligators and also Alphabets.* Oxford University Press, 1990.

Peet, Bill. *Zella, Zack and Zodiac.* Houghton Mifflin Company, 1986.

Name _____

Phonics Activity

Color the pictures that begin with the **Z** sound.

Zz

ZOO BARN

Zed Zebra

Zebra Pattern

Colors: Black
White

Needs: Eyes

Basic Body: White
(See page 8 for directions.)

O

Nostrils
Cut 2 White

Face Stripes
Cut 1 Black

Forelock
Cut 1 Black

Ears
Cut 2 Black

Neck Stripes
Cut 2 Black

Position the face stripes, ears, and forelock in place. The wide end of the forelock will be even with the top of the basic body. Glue on remaining features following illustration.

Alphabet Activities

Reproduce and use the letters on pages 141-144 in your classroom. Some ideas are given below.

- Children can use them to make their own alphabet books. They color and cut them out, then glue them to a page. They can then use pictures they've drawn or cut from magazines to represent those letters. This is a good homework activity.

- Use the letters on your bulletin board. They may be reproduced to use as titles for displays.

- Make several sets of the letters. Place them at a center. Have children use the letters to create words.

- Use the letters to make a matching game. Have students match the upper case letters to the lower case letters.

- Play concentration using the letters. Make two copies of each letter, cut them apart, and mix them up. Place them face down. Have students take turns picking up two at a time to find matches.

- Mix the letters up and have children arrange them in the correct order.

- Assign each child a different letter of the alphabet. Mix the letters, and choose them randomly to call on children.

- Place the letters on the floor. Have each student stand behind the letter that his or her first name begins with.

- Label items in the classroom using the letters.

- Have students make "Alphabet Feelies" by adding texture to the letters. Have students spread glue on the letter, then add salt, egg shells, noodles, or any other texture.

- Use the letters to make phonics pages for the letter you are teaching or wish to review.

The Alphabet—Upper Case

The Alphabet—Upper Case

The Alphabet—Lower Case

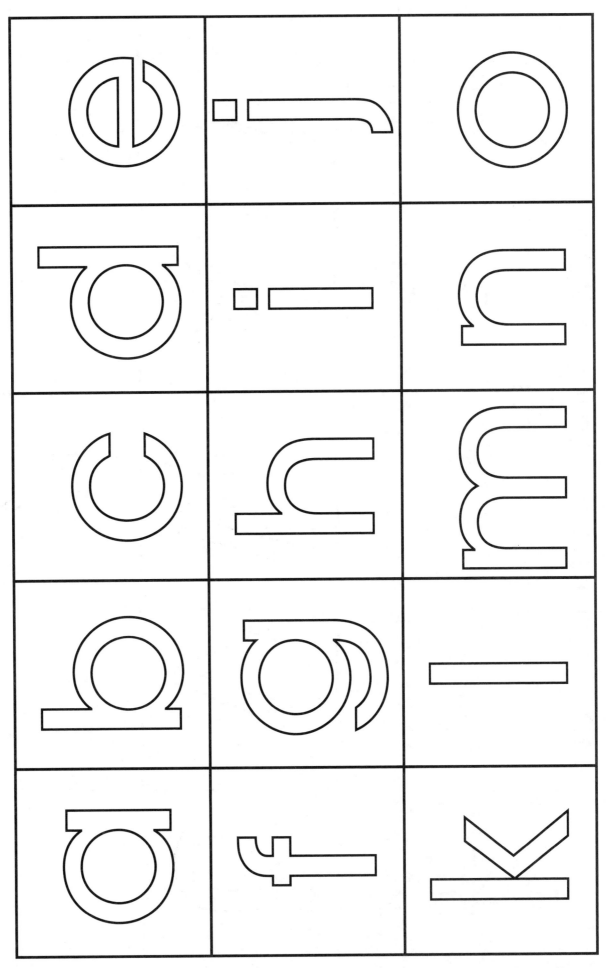

The Alphabet—Lower Case